Inspired to Action

Inspired to Action

How Young Changemakers Can Shape Their Communities and the World

Jean Rawitt

ROWMAN & LITTLEFIELD
Lanham • Boulder • New York • London

Published by Rowman & Littlefield
An imprint of The Rowman & Littlefield Publishing Group, Inc.
4501 Forbes Boulevard, Suite 200, Lanham, Maryland 20706
www.rowman.com

86-90 Paul Street, London EC2A 4NE, United Kingdom

British Library Cataloguing in Publication Information Available

Library of Congress Cataloging-in-Publication Data

Names: Rawitt, Jean, 1952– author.
Title: Inspired to action : how young changemakers can shape their communities and the world / Jean Rawitt.
Description: Lanham, Maryland : Rowman & Littlefield, [2023] | Includes bibliographical references and index. | Summary: "Inspired to Action provides concrete tools and resources to help young adults become skillful advocates who can work effectively to make real change happen. It includes sections on developing effective communication, fundraising, motivational skills, and more"—Provided by publisher.
Identifiers: LCCN 2022049697 (print) | LCCN 2022049698 (ebook) | ISBN 9781538169353 (Cloth) | ISBN 9781538169360 (epub)
Subjects: LCSH: Student movements—Handbooks, manuals, etc. | Youth—Political activity—Handbooks, manuals, etc. | Political activists—Handbooks, manuals, etc. | Social action—Handbooks, manuals, etc. | Motivation (Psychology)
Classification: LCC LA186 .R34 2023 (print) | LCC LA186 (ebook) | DDC 371.8/1—dc23/eng/20230118
LC record available at https://lccn.loc.gov/2022049697
LC ebook record available at https://lccn.loc.gov/2022049698

Contents

Introduction

"Each time that a man stands up for an ideal, or acts to improve the lot of others, or strikes out against injustice, he sends forth a tiny ripple of hope, and crossing each other from a million different centers of energy and daring, those ripples build a current that will sweep down the mightiest walls of oppression and resistance."[1]

—Robert F. Kennedy, Day of Affirmation Address,
University of Capetown, South Africa

If you are like almost every young person, your teenage years are a time of dramatic transformation: they are the years when kids turn into adults and when you must learn how to navigate and face the world in your new form. It is a time when you are probably facing disconcerting physical developments accompanied by volatile emotions, overwhelming stresses, passionate interests, intense friendships, and overall turbulence. At the same time, you are most likely trying to understand yourself, figuring out who you are and how you fit into your community, and perhaps trying to imagine what your future will be.

It can also be a time when you begin to develop and explore your own areas of interest in the larger world and when you can become powerfully drawn to causes and issues that capture your attention. This is often when young adults begin to recognize and respond to the inequities and injustice they see in the world, whether in their own neighborhoods, on social media, or in the news. You may find yourself becoming more tuned in to such things as the imbalances of social structure and the vast difference between wealth and poverty. You may become more aware of political factions and political actions, and begin to recognize and feel alarmed and even despairing about local and global issues like climate change, environmental pollution, religious freedom, homelessness, hunger, sexual and gender issues, animal rights, and unequal access to healthcare. Sometimes a local or world crisis stirs you to a powerful and immediate response, and sometimes a profound and deep interest develops over time. And for you, like for many other young people, the urge to act, to support and propel action, and even to instigate action becomes almost overwhelming. That urge to *do something* can be powerful and of enormous value if harnessed and deployed effectively. And that youthful, intense impulse to act can lead to positive, meaningful, and even hugely impactful change for the good.

However, just *wanting* to do something good is not enough to make it happen. There are many ways that you can do good work: you can choose to do volunteer service, fundraising for a worthy cause, or make personal donations of money or goods. As Mary Pipher wrote in an essay in the *New York Times*, "Most of us cannot be great heroes. However, we all have the capacity to be ordinary heroes. We may not be able to stop the global use of plastics, but we can work with local environmental groups. We cannot eliminate prejudice or nuclear weapons. However, we can deliver Meals on Wheels or repair bikes for giveaway programs."[2] Such individual good work can be of great value to the people who benefit from it, as well as an opportunity for deep personal gratification for those who perform it, and as Mary Pipher notes, any one of us can find ways to do good.

But while many young people find ways to serve, some teens find that their involvement and passion for a cause drive them to find ways to expand their role beyond themselves, to spread the word, and to influence and motivate others to join their cause and maximize the message and action. These young people become *activists*—they not only throw themselves into service, but they engage and mobilize others, propelling a groundswell of action that—when successful—can have enormous power to effect positive change.

One writer, Emmaline Soken-Huberly, recently highlighted the power of activism: "Whenever there's a positive change in society, we can thank activists. They work in every corner of the world on issues like racial justice, gender discrimination, and the countless intersections of social issues . . . Visions and specific goals vary, but activists want a better world."[3]

Activism can take many forms; it can involve protests, demonstrations, and marches. It can be workers—or students—going on strike. Civil disobedience—often referred to as nonviolent civil disobedience—is a form of activism. Also called passive resistance, civil disobedience is the refusal to obey the demands or commands of a government or occupying power without resorting to violence or active measures of opposition.[4] Activism can be door-to-door canvassing. Boycotting goods, services, or anything else is activism. And activism can take place through the use of communication, whether in a letter-writing campaign, petitions, or using social media to raise awareness of issues and mobilize as many people as possible in support of a single cause. Young people can be activists by educating others about an issue they care about; they can be advocates for legislation by working through their local government; and they can even run for elected office, whether in school government or on a larger stage.[5]

Young people have been forceful changemakers throughout the centuries—think of Tutankhamun, Alexander the Great, Joan of Arc, Louis Braille—these are just a few individuals who made their mark on the world before the age of twenty. More recently, teenagers were powerful agents of change in the labor and union movements of the early twentieth century, when they were instrumental in ending the exploitation of child labor. One of the most famous youth-led movements for positive change was the newsboys strike of 1899, which erupted after the two major New York newspapers raised their wholesale price, causing newsboys—who were essential to newspaper distribution—to pay more for each newspaper they sold. The newsboys declared a strike and—using methods including distributing flyers and protest signs, making some passionate speeches, and even the use of violence—eventually won their fight to get the prices lowered.[6] Later in the century, the civil rights movement of the 1960s brought many children, teenagers, and young adults to activism, not only attending meetings and marches, but braving violence to fight for equality in education and other aspects of society.[7] The stories of all those young people and those of more contemporary young people like Malala Yousafzai, Greta Thunberg, and X González (born Emma González), along with less well known teens who have also been responsible for extraordinary achievements, offer examples and inspiration for young people who feel moved to activism. Taking a look at the stories of these young people in later chapters can offer you guidance and role models, and demonstrates the breadth and scope of their different interests, as well as how they succeeded in doing remarkable things.

The past few years have seen a powerful surge in young people organizing to work for social change. The demonstrations against gun violence which spread across the country following the shooting at Marjory Stoneman Douglas High School; the Black Lives Matter marches following George Zimmerman's acquittal in the death of Trayvon Martin; the resurgence of the Black Lives Matter movement after the violent deaths of Michael Brown, Eric Garner, George Floyd, and too many others; and the climate change strikes and demonstrations around the world along with other actions driven largely by young people are clear evidence that young people collectively have a powerful voice, as well as the passion and energy to drive dynamic and forceful movements.

But to keep a forward momentum going and to spark new initiatives to make the world better, we need a continuing stream of activated and engaged young people to make action happen. They need to be inspired and encouraged to work for positive change, and they need to be empowered to do that effectively and sustainably so that their efforts can make a difference now and into the future.

Successful activism takes more than passion; it takes work, skills, commitment, and endless energy. There are ways to channel and deploy good intentions effectively, to inspire and engage others in the cause you care about so that your energy and enthusiasm become a force that is larger than yourself. Enthusiasm alone is not sufficient to effect positive change; you must learn to be thoughtful, strategic, well informed, articulate, diplomatic, and self-controlled so that your message, your passion, and your energy are focused and tuned for maximum results.

As Robert Kennedy said in his speech in Capetown, actions to improve the lives of others send forth ripples of hope. Hope is the feeling that allows you to envision something better, even when the odds seem overwhelming. When your goal is to work toward positive change, it is hope that fuels your work, drives your passion, and gives you the energy to continue despite setbacks, challenges, and all the obstacles you might face. But when you manage and deploy your strengths successfully with intention, integrity, and hope, you will find yourself better able to confront the suffering and damage in the world with action and determination rather than with despair.

At an education conference in 2011, the Dalai Lama asked people in the audience what they thought was the biggest threat to our world. He got a wide range of responses from his audience, who mentioned such threats as nuclear weapons, global poverty, and the environment. To those, the Dalai Lama responded by saying, "The greatest threat to our world is that we are raising a generation of passive bystanders."[8] That may have been true in 2011, but I believe that the past few years have proven that many of today's teens are bursting to take a stance, raise their voices, and throw themselves into taking action to create social change. Youth action is critical; young people—teens like you—hold the power to make positive change, but the key to doing that is taking action with effectiveness and determination, as well as refusing to stand by passively and wait for others to do it.

When is the right time to start taking action? The answer to that is *now*; now is always the right time to do good. "Some young people want to start out doing something," Katie Eder, an experienced young activist, told me, "But they feel they might say the wrong thing, or they're not educated enough, or they don't have the experience to do so. But there's no perfect time to start; just do it, just get involved, put your toe in, and then, once you're in a little bit, you can get more and more involved. You don't have to let it take over your whole life; you can make it work for you in the way you need it to."

My goal with this book is to provide some concrete tools and resources to help you get started or become a more skillful advocate, someone who can work effectively to make meaningful change happen, whatever the area of your interest. I hope you will be inspired and informed by the personal stories of some contemporary young change-makers, both famous and less well known, and gain insight from their stories of what motivated them to do the remarkable things they did and how they achieved their goals. Their accomplishments can provide roadmaps for you to create your own success.

You can gain tremendous benefits by learning to advocate effectively. The obvious one is that the cause you believe in and work to promote will gain from your involvement. But there are other, more personal benefits. There are powerful lessons you can learn when you are inspired to action. Learning to be an effective speaker, to organize your thoughts, to work collaboratively with others, to research deeply and understand a subject you are passionate about, and to advocate for yourself and for a cause you believe in—these are all transferable skills you can use no matter what you do, and they are valuable stepping-stones to gaining confidence and maturity, which will, hopefully, last a lifetime.

There are countless causes in the world which need your support, and there are others which have not yet surfaced but will undoubtedly make themselves known in the years to come. Today there is a tidal wave of issues which demand our attention and our action, and it will be young people—people like you—who will be leading the way forward. Whether it is fighting poverty or homelessness, gun violence or racism, or any one of the myriad other issues which may capture your attention, and whether you organize or communicate or raise funds or advocate, the power of your energy, your enthusiasm, your commitment, and your courage can be a force that helps shape positive change, whether on a small scale or a large one. Take the step, find your passion, and get involved. With the right tools and some guidance and encouragement, you can harness your own innate energy, enthusiasm, and determination and become an effective, powerful, confident advocate, a young person who might just have the power to change the world for the better.

Finally, a personal note: Over the past few years, I've often found myself feeling pessimistic and even despairing about the future of the world. The terrifying and rapid evolution of climate change, the ravages of war, the desperate hunger and poverty throughout the world's population, and diseases that spread faster and more virulently than ever all shake my faith that mankind and the planet will survive beyond the next few decades. But as I talked to young changemakers in this country and abroad and learned about the remarkable and creative ways they are addressing these and other overwhelming problems, and as I listened to their stories and saw the determination, the seriousness, and the intensity with which they were pursuing their projects and their ideals, I was inspired to optimism. In the hands of these outstanding young people and the many others like them throughout the world, I feel renewed confidence that these seemingly insurmountable problems which threaten our planet and the people on it will be mitigated, if not solved; with these young people, and all those like them—and you—I trust that we are in good hands.

Chapter One

Why Teens Can Be Powerful Agents of Change

There are certain characteristics inherent to youth that make teens, in some ways, even more effective activists than adults. Teens are more likely to be brash, headstrong, and impulsive, and they are generally more willing to take risks than older people.[1] They usually have more energy and enthusiasm than adults, are more willing to try new things, and very often think that they know more than they actually do, which can lead them to speak up and put themselves forward. Teens are prone to challenge things they find objectionable and usually express their views freely. Teens are rarely hesitant to show their passion for something—and passion can be infectious. Teens today also have tremendous potential to promote change through their vast and far-flung social networks, as well as the facility and nimbleness to use them effectively to influence others. Although all these traits can sometimes lead to unfortunate results (especially because teens are not known for always thinking through the potential consequences of their actions), they can also lead teens to accomplish change in unexpected and expansive ways.

There are important reasons why young people *should* become activists. As a recent Tufts University article on youth civic engagement states, "Young people have a massive stake in the decisions that shape the country. Nearly all issues affect youth, and many affect youth differently or uniquely: education, healthcare, the environment, immigration, housing, gun violence, and foreign policy that may send them or their peers to war."[2] And while those issues affect older people as well, teens will have many more years—perhaps even seventy or eighty more years beyond their teens—to deal with their consequences. Therefore, it is to your advantage to put your voice and your energy into ensuring that policies are put in place that will shape the results you would hope to see.

Activism and civic engagement are also *good* for teens. For example, in an article in the *New York Times*, writer Lisa Damour points to a study published in the journal *Child Development* which finds that "late adolescents and young adults who voted, volunteered or engaged in activism ultimately went further in school and had higher incomes than those who did not mobilize for political or social change."[3]

But even without knowing the benefits, young people have thrown themselves wholeheartedly into creating social change, and for hundreds of years, teens and young adults have proven they have the power to be effective activists. In an article about youth activism in America, Teena Apeles traces a long history of how youth have challenged and transformed our democracy, from young women working in textile mills in New England in 1834 who organized, demonstrated, and went on strike, eventually forming the first women's labor union, to more recent instances of youth activism, including protesting segregation, the Vietnam War, and gun violence and supporting immigration reform and the Black Lives Matter movement. "The youth of today are mobilized more than ever, especially in the age of social media," she writes. "They are continuing to fight for the same or similar issues their predecessors did . . . They are the future—and they will fight to have a say in it, as they have for the last two centuries. As one protest poster by a teenage girl read at the Youth Climate Strike in 2019: 'Hey adults, we'll take it from here.'"[4]

While young people are by no means a unified entity—teens certainly don't all think alike—they can offer a unique perspective on issues, and they can be an inexhaustible source of energy and passion for social change.[5] Those factors, in and of themselves, make young people a valuable resource in the world of social activism.

Older activists with years of experience recognize the power which young people have to be agents of change, especially when they organize to work together. For example, as Heather Booth, called by political journalist David Wood "one of the nation's most influential organizers for progressive causes,"[6] told me, "Almost every positive progressive social change movement in this country has been led by young people. Think about Black Lives Matter; the fight for a fifteen dollar minimum wage; the fight to unionize; and the fight for the environment; the truth is that there are millions of young people taking action. Look at the Dreamers, the fight for immigration reform; these young people in many states have won the right to have a public education *because they organized,* because people have taken action together."

Recent circumstances have also led young people to become more involved in social and political change for other reasons. Wisdom Cole, national director of the NAACP Youth and College Division, has an explanation for why in the past few years we have seen a particularly energized rise in the number of youthful activists:

During this global pandemic, we saw many young people working within our election system, working the polls, for example. Normally it would be a lot of older folks who would work the polls, but during the pandemic, many of them did not want to risk exposure to the virus. So young people stepped up; they became poll watchers, and poll workers, and canvassers, and took on the different roles that are necessary for upholding our democracy. And they did this because they believed in change, and believed that they had a role, a space, and a place in making that change.

In an address to the Economic and Social Council Youth Forum on "Youth Taking Action to Implement the 2030 Agenda" several years ago, UN Deputy Secretary-General Jan Eliasson strongly urged young people to take action for social change.

Far too often, young people have been side-lined from decision making, have had little or no say over the course of policies and actions that affect them. This has, for far too many young people, led to frustration and hopelessness, particularly if they are also facing persistent unemployment. This situation must change. Young people must be recognized for who they, you, are: agents of change whose contributions will bring

Canvassing means approaching people directly to solicit their votes, opinions, or support. Canvassers might go from house to house or stand on a street or in front of a shop or other public venue in an effort to speak to people directly.

benefits both to themselves—yourselves—and to society . . . We need you to engage in and share life-changing projects at the grassroots level. We look to you to work with local leaders, to advocate for action . . . We rely on you to be initiators and innovators, to be sources of knowledge and trailblazers for action.[7]

When teens begin to recognize and understand the role that they can play in making meaningful change, their power—especially when it is organized—can be significant. As Wisdom Cole explains, that power can be best developed through the effective use of politics, particularly local politics.

Young people are beginning to recognize that they have more power than they think they do. They are beginning to understand that the people who make the key decisions are elected by the people. Therefore, if they want to see the face of democracy change, they need to see people from their community, people who look like them, who come from similar experiences, and who hold similar values, get elected to positions of power. But to make that happen, you need to be part of that process, and you can do that even if you are too young to vote. That means developing relationships with elected officials, and letting them know that either they keep the issues most important to you at the top of their ticket, or they will be voted out.

And while you may think it is unlikely that you can have any political influence as a teenager, Wisdom Cole thinks otherwise. Wisdom points out the following:

When young people start locally, that is where they often begin to make a difference; for a lot of young people, getting involved in local elections is their first step. Local elections *matter*; when people, especially young people, can become involved within their communities, and influence how things happen locally, they see for themselves that the system can work. For many young people, that's the moment when it becomes more than just participating in one event, or doing it for just one season; it's the moment when they recognize that the work they are doing has the potential to transform lives for the better.

For Wisdom Cole, the message is clear:

Freedom is a constant struggle, something that we must constantly work for, something that we are constantly developing. But for us to really achieve freedom, young people have to be in the center of the movement. Young people have to be actively engaged, because the second that we remove young people from the process is the second we begin to lose our direction, because we need young people to constantly fuel our movement with new ideas. And I think everybody has their place in that movement, even if you think you don't. Whether it's going to a protest, or being a policy writer, or answering phones, we can all play our part and work together. It's important to think about how you can use your talent, your tools, your time, and your treasure to work with others towards a common goal, a common good.

"Adolescents need to experience a sense of belonging and purpose," says Nancy Deutsch, an education professor and director of the University of Virginia Curry School of Education's Youth-Nex Center to Promote Effective Youth Development. "Youth are not only our future, they are actively shaping our world today. Young people have a long history of being on the vanguard of social change movements. Across the globe, young people are on the front lines of social change. This can be tremendously positive." Professor Deutsch continues, "For example, great forward movement in our society around issues of race, gender and sexuality have been driven by the activism of youth." Dr. Deutsch points to the efforts of trans youth whose activism pushed schools to look at their policies surrounding issues related to gender identification and access to bathroom and locker rooms. "And today, more than ever, with the rise and impact of social media," says Dr. Deutsch, "The power of youth to make their voices heard and shape political debates is great."[8]

For some teens, though, even the *idea* of being able to be an effective changemaker is not something they are able to contemplate, even if they think there is something they want to do. As one young changemaker, Russell Agustin, has explained, "Some of my peers see social change as something up on a pedestal, something that only a rare few can achieve. They learn about these amazing historical figures who contributed to the development of our society, and that seems so far from what they can ever imagine doing that it creates a barrier to believing that they can actually contribute personally to social change." But while there are certainly those rare young people who have achieved worldwide fame for their activism—like Malala Yousafzai and Greta Thunberg—there are many, many more teens who have made significant impact on their communities and beyond through resourcefulness, ingenuity, organization, and the power of dogged determination.

Even so, as Wisdom Cole points out, it is all too easy to become frustrated.

Many people, perhaps especially young people, are passionate about a cause, and they may hear those in power promise to do something about it, but then it seems that nothing gets done, and so they get fed up with a political system that they feel is not working, is corrupt, and uses compromise in place of action. Young people often think that compromise is a dirty word, and that you can't make significant change within the slow movement of the democratic process, that change only happens with revolutionary change. But in recent years, young people have begun to see that—particularly on social media—influencers can be very powerful in moving public opinion to put pressure on elected officials.

Heather Booth reiterated why young people can be powerful agents of change. "We can't underestimate the power of young people," she has reminded me.

With the Black Lives Matter movement, it was young people who started the cry, "Hands up, Don't Shoot!" And with that cry they attracted the attention of the country—and of the world—through the use of social media. That wasn't an old person's idea—it was young people who did it. Young people can take bold action, in part because they usually don't have the responsibilities which older people may. They have greater freedom than older people, so they're willing to take more risks. And because they aren't tied to doing things the way they've always been done, they are able to come up with more creative ideas than older people might. Young people bring creativity, courage, and inventiveness to action, and *that* makes progress.

Chapter Two

Twelve Young Changemakers

Who They Are and How They Make Things Happen

There are many young activists who have, in the past few years, received worldwide recognition and acclaim. You've certainly heard about some of them: one of the best known is Malala Yousafzai, who won the Nobel Peace Prize for her brave and tireless fight for the right of every child to receive an education. Greta Thunberg is another; her decision to begin a solo school strike for climate action launched the international movement Fridays for Future, raising worldwide awareness of climate change and spurring young people across the globe to take action in following her lead. X González (formerly known as Emma González) and her fellow activists from Marjory Stoneman Douglas High School in Parkland, Florida, rallied thousands of people across the country and around the world through March for Our Lives protests for gun control. While still in their teens, these young people brought tremendous visibility to their causes and have served as role models for young people everywhere. Their stories are remarkable, and their accomplishments are truly inspiring. But there are many young activists less well known who are taking action in all sorts of ways and for a multitude of causes, whose stories are just as inspiring. These young people offer lessons from their own experience that can help anyone on the road to becoming a changemaker. Reading about these young people and others like them will give you a sense of the breadth of their interests and passions and, perhaps, help you pursue your own.

I spoke with young activists in the United States and elsewhere in the world to find out about their journeys—what brought them to activism, what kept them going, what they've accomplished, and what they've learned along the way. They are each extraordinary in their own fashion, but they are alike in their passion to work toward making the world a better, more equitable, and more loving place. There is a lot to be learned from their experiences, and you can learn more about them—and from them—throughout the book. But first, let's take a look at who they are and how they got started taking action to solve social problems.

RUSSELL AGUSTIN: *CONNECTING SUSTAINABILITY AND HEALTHY LIVING THROUGH COMMUNITY*

Founder, Sole2Soul

Russell Agustin is a young man whose path to activism began with an actual road trip—a family road trip to see America. During the trip, while on a visit to an Indian reservation, Russell found himself deeply disturbed by the poor living conditions he saw there. Already interested in the environment, the conditions he saw planted in his mind the idea of trying to find a way to bring people and the planet together and, at the same time, highlight the importance of community in bringing about environmental change.

While still a freshman in high school, Russell built on that idea. He focused on the fact that while many young people in low-income communities did not have adequate footwear to participate in sports or other activities, elsewhere, perfectly good athletic shoes were often tossed aside when outgrown or when interest in the sport had faded. Russell decided to develop a program that would bring need and resource together and put athletic shoes on the feet of kids who needed them. In

---

Articles of incorporation refers to a legal document that you are required to file with your state government if you intend to incorporate your business.[*]

---

[*] "What Are Articles of Incorporation?" ContractsCounsel, accessed June 19, 2022, https://www.contractscounsel.com/t/us/articles-of-incorporation.

his sophomore year, Russell filed articles of incorporation to establish a nonprofit organization he called Sole2Soul, with the goal of promoting sustainability and healthy living through the collection, reuse, and repurposing of athletic shoes.[1] Since its founding, Sole2Soul has distributed shoes in Nigeria, Kenya, the Philippines, and the Bay Area of California.

Russell, now studying at University of Southern California, is committed to making changemaking more accessible for everyone. Early in his journey as an activist, Russell became involved in Ashoka, an organization founded in 1980 by Bill Drayton and based on the idea that the most powerful force for good in the world is social entrepreneurship. Working within Ashoka's changemaker network, Russell actively promotes the Ashoka concept: "Everyone a Changemaker." He is the founder and CEO of Tilt Consultancy, which launched Tilt Camp, an entrepreneurship camp aimed at empowering young people to start their own projects.

Although Russell did establish his own nonprofit organization, he points out that it is not necessary to do that in order to become involved in making change. In fact, he stresses several benefits for young people in joining an already established organization tied to your interests: "For most people," Russell says, "joining an organization that is mission-aligned with your values can lead you to a space of inclusivity, collaboration, and acceptance, and allows you to be part of something that is bigger than yourself."

For Russell, getting started in the world of nonprofits meant starting from the beginning.

> There is no shame in saying that the first mentor who really brought me into the concept of entrepreneurship and building initiatives with social impact was my mom. When my peers—and even some of my family—doubted my ability to create something like Sole2Soul, it was my mom who pushed me to start things off. Later, I had some business mentors, but before I had them, I had Google. I think our generation is privileged to have something like Google, a search engine which really leads you almost anywhere. For instance, I knew nothing about how to start a nonprofit corporation, so I googled "How to start a nonprofit" on WikiHow, and that's literally where it started.

"A *nonprofit organization* is one that qualifies for tax-exempt status by the IRS [Internal Revenue Service] because its mission and purpose are to further a social cause and provide a public benefit."*

---

* Emily Heaslip, "Nonprofit vs. Not-for-Profit vs. For-Profit: What's the Difference?" US Chamber of Commerce, published April 20, 2021, https://www .uschamber.com/co/start/strategy/nonprofit-vs-not-for-profit-vs-for-profit.

Russell went on to get training and mentorship through a local organization, Youth Impact Hub of Oakland, as well as through Ashoka, T-Mobile, and his own high school.

The role of mentors has been monumental for me, not just for the learning basis, but for the networking. My business teacher in high school used to say, "Sometimes it's not what you know, but who you know, and how you know them," and that's been the case for me.

A big issue for teens is that we feel we know everything. And sometimes that leads us to make mistakes. But a mentor can help us look at our mistakes as avenues and opportunities to learn, and when we open the door to accepting someone else's wisdom and someone else's perspective, that's incredibly valuable.

I also think it's important for young people to keep in mind, when they're starting a project, that nothing will ever go according to plan. In fact, I think that's an absolute: nothing will ever go according to plan. So you have to get used to being open to adjusting and adapting your plans. And you need to know that if Plan A doesn't work, there are other letters in the alphabet. I've seen some young activists meet with their first set of obstacles, and then they think, well, that's the end of the line, my work stops here. But you need to be able to use failure as a tool to learn. You have to get comfortable with the uncomfortable. You have to get used to criticism, and obstacles, and failure, and find ways to keep going on. There's a phrase that's always in my mind, that keeps me going: "Adversity is to be expected, but curiosity needs to be maintained."

Russell also speaks about another issue common to teens:

What have I learned, what might I have done differently, in starting Sole2Soul? I think I would have asked for more help, and I should have been more open to criticism and feedback. In the beginning, I was very territorial about my work, very protective of my idea. And I think that kind of overprotectiveness restricted who I let get involved with the work I was doing. It also cut off a lot of the mentorship that I probably could have had, if only I had reached out. So, when I think about it, I think that if I could turn back the hands of time, I would probably have asked for more help.

WISDOM COLE: *FROM INDIVIDUAL ACTIVIST TO TRAINING YOUNG ACTIVISTS NATIONWIDE*

National Director of NAACP Youth and College Division

In a few short years, Wisdom Cole's personal journey in the world of activism has taken him from action to youth leadership; he is now the director of the Youth and College Division of the NAACP.[2] In that role he works with youth councils of high school and college students actively involved in the fight for civil rights. He has been widely featured in the media as an advocate for Black youth voter turnout and grassroots organizing and has received many awards for his achievements.

Wisdom told me the following:

I started my journey in activism when I was in college at the University of California, Santa Cruz, in 2013, and a not-guilty verdict was announced in George Zimmerman's trial for the murder of Trayvon Martin. It seemed like the University administration was turning a blind eye to that event, and those of us on campus who were deeply disturbed by what was happening wanted a statement from the University about the issue. We felt that we needed to take to the streets to show that business as usual couldn't continue: there was the loss of a Black life, and the killer was going unpunished. It was during these demonstrations and protests that I recognized the power of community action and that being able to really educate people, not just for a day but for an entire lifetime, could be transformative.

It's always been important for me to learn lessons from my elders; I believe those lessons can inform the future. My gateway into activism and organizing was University of California, Santa Cruz, which has a history

of activism from its inception and offered so many opportunities to learn
from powerful activists. When I look back on my life, I realize how lucky
I am to have been able to hear directly from some of the folks who created the Black Power movement and to interact with them. I've had conversations with Bobby Seale, cofounder of the Black Panther Party. I've
sat down with Elaine Brown, the first female chair of the Black Panther
Party, and been able to hear her story and hear how the movement came
to be, how they organized. Angela Davis is a professor emerita there, and
I've had multiple opportunities to interact with her, to hear from her, and
even be mentored by her. And I know how lucky I am to have had these
opportunities. Learning from these people, I recognized how important
it is to learn from our history, otherwise we continue to repeat the same
things over and over again. I'm always looking for ways in which we can
learn from our past and find ways to improve.

JONAH DOCTER-LOEB: *PUTTING TECHNOLOGY TO CREATIVE USE IN A PANDEMIC*

Founder, Print to Protect

For Jonah Docter-Loeb, there are distinct personal rewards for working
on a project he is passionate about. Jonah talked openly with me about
why being involved in a social impact project is so meaningful for him.

As a senior in high school, Jonah launched Print to Protect[3] during
the early days of the pandemic, after being galvanized by seeing news
reports of healthcare workers struggling to care for patients without
having adequate personal protective equipment (PPE). A 3-D printer
enthusiast, Jonah's idea was to make plastic face shields for medical
workers using an online design and his own 3-D printer. Within a short
time, Jonah had recruited a network of dozens of people with 3-D print-
ers to begin to make protective face shields in quantity for healthcare
workers while commercially produced PPE was in short supply, with
additional volunteers lined up to assemble and distribute them where
needed.

> When I'm involved in a project, the core for me is that I'm at my best
> when I'm working on something, putting my all into a project and having
> the opportunity to feel that I'm helping someone else. But I also know that
> I am helping myself and growing personally through that process. When
> I throw myself into a project, it enhances my own learning; I take classes

formatted around my interest, and how it relates to the project I'm working on, and I think about everything through that framework. I do feel, though, that's something of a selfish motivation, because I enjoy focusing on a project. I really feel that I get energy from it, and I know that I'm at my best when I'm busy managing teams, putting together a passion project, or working on something that I'm excited about.

The other side for me is a certain sense of obligation, knowing that I come from a privileged and fortunate background. I am lucky to have so many connections and opportunities that many other people don't have, especially at my age, and I feel that it is a duty to put them to use for something good. That's always been a core motivation for me.

Even before he founded Print to Protect, Docter-Loeb was drawn toward activism by several forces. The first is that he comes from a family with a tradition of political and social impact engagement, so choosing to become involved in a social impact project felt familiar. He also found an early and important influence toward activism in the world of speech and debate. As he says, "Being exposed to a community of people trying to be persuasive, to stand up for things, or just arguing for fun really exposed me to a group of people who were civically minded and were active in one way or another, even if that way of being active was just having knowledge of what is going on in the world."

"One of the foundational things I've learned through doing these projects," Jonah said, "is to have increased confidence. To pursue ideas, to take myself seriously—sometimes too seriously—and to speak my mind, to investigate things, and even to resolve interpersonal conflicts; these were tremendously important things I've been able to learn through this experience. That, and learning how to think about where and how I've been wrong, and how I could do things better next time;

Social impact means "any significant or positive changes that solve or at least address social injustice and challenges."*

---

* Nicole Mitchell, "Social Impact: Definition and Why Is Social Impact Important?" Duke Career Hub, published September 3, 2021, https://careerhub .students.duke.edu/blog/2021/09/03/social-impact-definition-and-why-is-social -impact-important/.

that is a difficult thing to do, but I know I've had real growth in that regard."

KATIE EDER: *CONNECTING YOUNG ACTIVISTS ACROSS THE COUNTRY*

Cofounder, 50 Miles More

For Katie Eder, now an influential and effective leader in the world of youth activism, "the word activism, or organizing, was never on my radar as a child. I didn't have any frame of reference for it, but I did grow up in the Jewish community and, early on, learned a basic value: when there are problems, we need to help solve those problems. There is a Hebrew phrase, *tikkun olam*, which basically means to repair the world. The whole sentiment is that we, as a people, have an obligation to other people and to the planet to help make the world better and to help repair what's broken."

Katie has been an ardent force in youth activism since her very early teens in Madison, Wisconsin. Her first venture was founding Kids Tales, a series of creative writing workshops taught by teens for kids who did not have access to writing experiences outside of school. Then, following the March for Our Lives protests against gun violence in 2018, Katie and peers from her high school organized a fifty-mile march from Madison to Janesville, Wisconsin, the home-town of former Speaker of the House Paul Ryan, protesting his role in blocking gun legislation. That led Katie and her team to launch 50 Miles More, which challenged every state to hold similar fifty-mile marches with the goal of forcing legislation to end gun violence. Through this experience, Katie forged alliances with other youth-led organizations around the country, resulting in her forming Future Coalition,[4] a national network and community of young people work-ing together to make the future a better, safer, and more equitable place for everyone.

The impetus for founding Future Coalition, says Katie, came out of the climate strikes and the youth climate movement. "The question became, how do we ignite the amount of energy we saw happening around the strikes, and how do we sustain it? And one of the things we're coming to realize is that we need to activate new young people, and we need to bring in new young people. One of the centerpieces of our strategy with Future Coalition is inspiration empowerment: how do we reach young people who we are not reaching and inspire them in a way that they weren't before?"

For Katie—who, when we spoke, was busy putting together the first retreat for her team since the beginning of the pandemic—the focus has been on relationship building.

It's the first time a lot of us are meeting in person, and obviously, there's a lot of nervousness around that. But as we built the agenda, it was a great feeling to know that we were building the agenda together, prioritizing being together, prioritizing our relationship building. We felt that, at this point, relationship building was the most important thing. Putting together this retreat showed the importance of relationship building, of building trust, building community, and doing something together. It may take more time to get that buy-in from different people, but when you're able to do that, it's just so much more powerful, so much more effective. And one thing that I've really learned doing this is that you have to lean on the people around you and trust people and build those relationships so that you can divide the work, and you can divide the pressure, and the responsibility, and the excitement, and the good parts so that you're sharing with other people. To me that is just so, so critical.

I asked Katie, a sophomore in college when we spoke, what she envisioned doing in the future.

Before the 2020 election, I had never thought about that question. I had no ability to think past the 2020 election, so I didn't really think about planning what I would do in the future. I'm an American Studies student at Stanford now, and my concentration is Transforming the American Political System, a huge concentration, but I think it represents what I hope to do. I don't necessarily see myself running for office, but I do think

Buy-in is typically used to mean "acceptance of and willingness to actively support and participate in something."*

---

* "Buy-in," *Merriam-Webster Dictionary*, accessed June 21, 2022, https://www.merriam-webster.com/dictionary/buy-in.

that America as a democracy, a democratic republic as we know it today, is not going to be what it is in fifteen or twenty years. I think there will be some sort of large change, some sort of revolutionary-style change in the systems that exist in this country, and I would love to be engaged in part of that. I'm not quite sure yet what that role might look like, but I hope to be doing something like that.

KAKOOZA HAKIM: *PUTTING HEALTHCARE INNOVATION INTO PRACTICE*

Cofounder, Aid You Project

Kakooza Hakim found his passion for social enterprise in Uganda, Africa. His efforts to create sustainable solutions to help underserved communities gain access to quality healthcare are very much driven by his personal experience.

After his father died suddenly of a heart attack when Kakooza was three years old, he grew up believing that his father's life might have been saved had there been local access to emergency medical care. At the age of fifteen, while studying robotics at a local nongovernmental organization (NGO), Kakooza got the idea to create something that people could use to get the medical attention they need in time. Because of his father's history, which led him to think about creating cost-friendly defibrillators (electronic devices to restart a failing heart) that could be located in remote areas far from medical centers, his hope was that, even if he could not have saved his father, he might save other lives.

Using their robotic skills, Kakooza and a young colleague created prototypes for just such a defibrillator but then realized they had to learn more about how and where they might be used. Kakooza wanted

---

Social enterprise refers to an activity undertaken by a nonprofit or a for-profit business or an individual that may yield both financial and social returns.*

---

* "What Is Social Enterprise?" Candid Learning, accessed June 21, 2022, https://learning.candid.org/resources/knowledge-base/social-enterprise/.

NGOs (or nongovernmental organizations) are generally "a voluntary group of individuals or organizations, usually not affiliated with any government, that is formed to provide services or to advocate a public policy. Although some NGOs are for-profit corporations, the vast majority are nonprofit organizations."[*]

---

[*] "Nongovernmental Organization," *Britannica,* accessed June 21, 2022, https://www.britannica.com/topic/nongovernmental-organization/.

to meet with doctors at the Ugandan Heart Institute to learn more from them about heart disease and what might best benefit underserved communities. With no experience setting up such a meeting, when he first showed up asking to speak with a doctor, he was turned away because he had not called in advance, and the staff did not take him seriously. Kakooza quickly realized he needed a better approach: he had to dress less like a student and more like an adult, and he would need to make an appointment and have an agenda for what he wanted to discuss. After having prepared a list of questions and a request for information, Kakooza returned to the Heart Institute and was successful in making an appointment to speak with a cardiologist. At their meeting Kakooza impressed the doctor with his serious intent and the research and engineering he had already done. The doctor invited several of his colleagues to also meet with Kakooza, and they undertook to help educate him about cardiology, heart disease, and the needs of cardiac patients, and to help him formulate a plan. With their guidance and mentorship, Kakooza became intrigued by the health needs of rural communities and soon realized that the biggest problem he needed to address was not a lack of defibrillators but a lack of basic health and medical information.

Kakooza and his colleague were able to secure a small grant from Peace First, which enabled them to survey and analyze community needs and then to begin work on addressing those needs. Their first step was to learn basic life support skills, including CPR (cardiopulmonary resuscitation), after which they developed a curriculum to train other students in how to perform such basic life support procedures. Since then, with this program, Kakooza and his colleague have trained more than 1,500 students in basic first aid and preventative healthcare

> *Social entrepreneurship*, according to the US Chamber of Com-
> merce, is "the process by which individuals, startups and entrepre-
> neurs develop and fund solutions that directly address social issues.
> A social entrepreneur, therefore, is a person who explores business
> opportunities that have a positive impact on their community, in
> society or the world."[*]
>
> ───────────
>
> [*] Sean Peek, "What Is Social Entrepreneurship? 5 Examples of Businesses with
> a Purpose," US Chamber of Commerce, published July 30, 2020, https://www
> .uschamber.com/co/start/startup/what-is-social-entrepreneurship/.

so that they could go out into remote communities and educate people
about heart-related illnesses common in those communities and preventative healthcare, such as how to adopt healthier diets. In 2021
Kakooza was recognized for his initiative with a Diana Award, given
to outstanding young people creating and sustaining positive social
change, named in memory of Princess Diana. An innovator and social
entrepreneur, Kakooza studies at Africa Leadership University and
continues to mentor other young activists as a program coordinator at
Tilt Consultancy.

MARY CATHERINE HANAFEE LAPLANTE: *ENVIRONMENTAL ACTIVISM AND BEYOND*

Founder, Speak Up Green Up

For Mary Catherine (MC) Hanafee LaPlante, an early interest in
ecological science was the avenue toward creating change in her community in Illinois. As a youngster, MC thrived while participating in
Science Olympiad, winning first in state and regional competitions
year after year. One day, playing softball in a local park, she noticed
groundskeepers spraying an exorbitant amount of pesticides not far
from areas where children were playing and dogs were sniffing everywhere. Horrified by what she saw and fascinated by ecological science,
she researched the harmful effects of pesticide use on people, animals,
and the environment. What she learned led her to focus her interest on

the issue of clean water and the need to eliminate the use of pesticides and herbicides that tainted the water in her community. Passionately driven to work toward eliminating the dangerous chemicals that were seeping into her neighborhood's water supply, she founded Speak Up Green Up,[5] a nonprofit, youth-led environmental organization focused on that goal.

MC's work with Speak Up Green Up and her science expertise and determined pursuit of the issue of pesticide contamination of the water supply led her to work with legislative officials to ban the use of those substances near parks and schools. Moving beyond that issue, she went on to become active in broader areas of student environmental activism, taking on a leadership role in the Illinois Youth Climate Movement, which organized massive strikes in Chicago, drawing attention to the negative impact of climate change.

However, MC's involvement in pursuing positive social change was not restricted to science and the environment; she soon turned her activism to the issue of menstrual equity—ensuring the affordability and accessibility of menstrual products and ending the stigma about menstruation—and organized the first Period Rally in Chicago, advocating for the availability of free menstrual products in schools, college dorms, and restrooms, as well as in prisons and homeless shelters. Her activism and visibility helped her connect with other programs, legislators, and, particularly, women leaders and enabled her to secure grants and funding for the work she was doing.

MC's parents were role models for her in the areas of social good, community involvement, and political activism. "Seeing them involved in anti-racism activities, environmental things like eliminating chemicals in the house, using organic foods, and just helping other people in the community definitely impacted me a lot," she says. "I think that any young person who gets involved in activism as a kid, it's very likely that they are surrounded by people they learn it from. It's such a niche path to take, it generally doesn't happen in a void." Now studying economics and government at Harvard, MC is looking ahead to how she will continue to work for change as her journey continues.

ZOYA HAQ: *PROMOTING LITERACY AND LEARNING WITH BOOKS AND STORYTELLING*

Founder, The Tahira Project

Zoya Haq became interested in the concept of educational equity when she was quite young. Inspired by her grandmother, Tahira Haroon, who was a writer throughout her lifetime and fostered Zoya's love of literature and learning, Zoya's goal became to connect other young people with the same educational opportunities her grandmother had been given. While still in middle school, Zoya decided to collect donated books from within her community and sell them, giving the money she raised to organizations in underserved areas supporting educational equity. She named her program the Tahira Project,[6] in memory of her grandmother.

> When I first got the idea for the Tahira Project, I was kind of rebellious and in the I-want-to-do-this-by-myself stage, so I didn't even tell my mother about it until a couple of weeks after I had started collecting books. I'd told all my friends about what I was going to do and asked them to spread the word and tell their families to bring donations of books to me. I started to reach out to more friends by text and reach out to community members as well, and then my mom just figured it out because people were dropping off boxes and boxes of books at our house, and suddenly it was, "What's going on?"
>
> But once I'd explained, my mom was really supportive and helped me scale it up. She helped me connect with people she knew, with family friends and acquaintances, and we got even more book donations. People were really supportive because a lot of people have books lying around the house which they don't read anymore and are happy

Scale, or *to scale up*: To scale your organization means to expand it. That is not as simple as just reaching out to more people or expanding your constituency. Successful scaling means making sure that you have planned appropriately for growth—that you have the support, the people, the technology, and the processes to grow without losing the ability to function or achieve your goals effectively.

to donate, so people would come by and drop off twenty or thirty books at a time.

In the beginning, I sold books in person because I wasn't very knowledgeable about setting up an online website; but once I realized how many people were buying books, I decided to create a website and sell books online. I'd created a website for our school newspaper in middle school, so I figured I'd create a website on Wix. I collected some donations of money from within our community and used those to build a website because Wix has a subscription fee, and I needed money to pay for that. After I did that, I set up an online bookstore and started blasting it out to friends all over the country, and soon, we started shipping books out nationally.

Before I started the Tahira Project, I was already involved with two organizations; one was the International Esperanza Project in Guatemala and one was the Citizens Foundation in Pakistan, which is where my family is from. We have a lot of family friends who are involved with the Citizens Foundation, which builds schools in Pakistan and helps pay tuition and transportation costs for kids to attend, so that was the first organization that I knew I wanted to donate money to. I went to a number of their events around Dallas and sold books there. People who attended the events knew I was raising money for the organization through book sales, so they were happy to buy books because they knew the money was going to a cause they supported. The International Esperanza Project was started by a close family friend from Guatemala, so I worked with her to help fund the El Molina School in Guatemala with money raised through the Tahira Project.

Zoya's success in this initial venture introduced her to the world of social impact and helped her gain confidence in her ability to carry out complex projects. While she was still in her sophomore year of high school, she and three friends launched her second project, HiStory Retold,[7] working to diversify the nation's educational curricula by providing teachers, students, parents, and community members with an online platform on which to share their stories.

For Zoya, the impetus for HiStory Retold came from her personal experience. As Zoya explains, "I began to realize that I was not seeing myself reflected in the curriculum. I know that's an issue for a lot of students nationwide, and it's something that can contribute to a lack of self-confidence and to the perpetuation of prejudice. I'm a huge fan of stories myself; I just really like to write, I like to learn from other people, I like to share my own story, and I know that other people like to share their stories as well. So I wanted to make sure that everyone has a platform to share their story within a scholastic environment."

HAYAT HASSAN: *BRINGING TUTORING AND ADVOCACY TO UNDERSERVED YOUTH*

Cofounder, Kow iyo Labo

Hayat Hassan arrived in the United States from Kenya when she was a young child, having made the hazardous journey with her mother and four siblings in the hope of finding a better, safer life. Growing up in a single-parent household and struggling financially, Hayat was inspired by her mother, who instilled in her children a social consciousness. As Hayat says, "The idea of social responsibility, of being responsible for creating a better world, was something that was ingrained in my upbringing."

Hayat's family settled in Minneapolis, where there were many other African immigrants. For Hayat's mother, who never had access to education, getting her children educated was a top priority. Hayat attended local charter schools in North Minneapolis during her early years but then entered a large public high school.

In high school, it quickly became clear to Hayat that her education had been sorely lacking; the charter schools—which mostly served children from disadvantaged communities—had been significantly underfunded, leaving them with few educational resources. As Hayat struggled to catch up in her new school, her realization that she had missed educational opportunities because of the lack of resources in her earlier schools and that the education system was not equal for all students was, as she says, "my very first wake up call."

While still in high school, Hayat, along with her older sister and one of her friends from school, founded Kow iyo Labo,[8] a tutoring and advocacy center for children. "I started Kow iyo Labo because, after we found ourselves falling behind in school just because of our educational background, we started thinking, 'If we're falling behind, so many other students must be going through this as well.'"

Kow iyo Labo has not been Hayat's only foray into the social impact sphere. During Hayat's junior year in high school, she lost her part-time job at a coffee shop when she was furloughed due to the pandemic. She

Advocacy is "the act or process of supporting a cause or proposal."*

* "Advocacy," *Merriam-Webster Dictionary*, accessed June 21, 2022, https://www.merriam-webster.com/dictionary/advocacy/.

had been working for several years already, helping contribute to her family's household finances, and the loss of her job hit hard. What hit harder was finding out that in Minnesota, high school students were not covered by unemployment insurance as adult workers were.

Hayat quickly connected through the internet with other Minnesota young people who had lost jobs, and they began to pursue reform efforts to change the law that was depriving them of unemployment benefits. This led them to a local nonprofit, Youthprise, which focused on addressing inequities facing low-income and racially diverse young people. Youthprise ultimately filed a federal lawsuit against the state Department of Employment and Economic Development for barring high school students from receiving CARES (Coronavirus Aid, Relief, and Economic Security Act) funds, to which older workers were entitled.

Hayat, a student at Harvard when we spoke, said that since childhood, she had imagined that she would study law and become a human rights lawyer but has now begun to rethink her future plans. "I am constantly evaluating what is the best way to bring about change, and at this moment, I don't think it's through our legal system, and it may not be through any system. Perhaps you need to be outside the system to disrupt the system. But I'm only a freshman in college, and I have so much learning to do before I know where I am going in the future."

JOÃO PEDRO LELLIS: *PROVIDING TECHNOLOGY TO DISADVANTAGED STUDENTS*

Cofounder, Athena Tech Project

A high school student in São Paolo, Brazil, João Pedro Lellis says he has always been very curious and a good student. For João Pedro, the internet and technology provided ready access to information and an easy way to further his knowledge and explore his curiosity. But as he grew up, he began to realize that there was a huge educational disparity in Brazil, as acceptance to national universities was based almost entirely on an exam, and young people who did not have access to all the educational resources and information available on the internet were therefore handicapped in their ability to do well on the test. While private schools such as those João Pedro attended were able to offer access to computers and the internet, public schools were lagging behind in being able to provide those tools. According to João Pedro, just prior to the pandemic, only 40 percent of students in public schools in Brazil had access to a device on which to use the internet. As his awareness of this disparity grew, so did João Pedro's impulse to find a way to expand opportunities for education through technology.

"My family wasn't really involved in activism," João Pedro told me. "So I basically had to find my own way. But the teachers in my school are very critical of society and talked a lot about social problems; they always encouraged us to think about things on a deeper level, below the surface. I think that definitely helped me become more critical in my thinking and more interested in trying to do something to make change happen."

João Pedro learned about Tilt Camp, an offshoot of Ashoka (which helps train young people to become effective changemakers), through his interest in studying abroad. Accepted as a participant, João Pedro and his group focused on developing a project which would make the internet more available to Brazilian public school students. João Pedro said the following:

> Initially, our idea was to donate computers to individuals, which is good; but then we realized that doing so wouldn't impact very many people, because if you donate ten computers, you are only helping ten people. Then we started thinking of a way to help more people, and we came up with the idea of setting up "learning pods," spaces in public schools or anywhere else that underprivileged students might have access to, and providing them with access to technology and the internet in those pods.
>
> We were able to make some connections with businesses which gave us donations, and we were able to set up two pods at an NGO which had an afterschool program for students. Then we were able to donate six computers to a public school which needed computers. Although the government had promised them computers, it was going to take months

or even a year to be able to get them through the government, so they were very grateful when we were able to provide them. Since then, we have worked towards getting more people involved and more companies involved, and really looking to scale our project in the next year.

I think that a lot of young people feel that they can't help, that they can't do something that is real and makes a difference, that they have to wait until they are older or graduate from college before they can do something that's really helpful in the world. But I think that working on my project, learning what I did at Tilt Camp, showed me that it's unnecessary to wait to reach a certain age.

My goal now is to get more young people involved to keep the education project going, especially before I go off to college and then start going to work, having a more adult schedule. But I also want to always stay involved, to work to keep it going, because I think that it is something useful, something good for other people. Even if it's not my full-time job, I want to always be able to engage in opportunities to help people. I always think about this one man I met, one of the partners in a company which helped us a lot, and he was just such a good mentor to me, teaching me a lot of things, giving resources and funding to our program, and really caring about what we are doing. And so that's the person I believe I want to be in the future: someone who helps other people, mentors other young people, gives opportunities to young people. If I have the resources, I want to help with the resources. If all I have is knowledge, I want to help with the knowledge. That's the person I would say I want to be.

GIOVANNA PIMENTEL: *FINDING HER OWN WAY IN THE WORLD OF ACTIVISM*

Codeveloper, EducaAid Project

In Giovanna Pimentel's experience, access to a culture of social impact and activism was not readily available to a young person in São Paolo, Brazil, where she is a high school student. "In Brazil, there's really a gap. To get into college in Brazil, you just have to do well on a test. We don't have anything here for someone like me, who is preparing to go to college in the United States, where so much of college acceptance is based on extracurricular activities, volunteer projects, and essays about things you have done. I think here in Brazil, students don't become involved in those kinds of activism projects, and they volunteer less than in other countries."

Giovanna's interests and passion focused on education and the environment. Even without being directly exposed to any kind of social activism, Giovanna knew that she wanted to do something in one or both of those areas, something that would help make the world a better place. She began to do research on her own, trying to find programs which hooked her interest and trying to figure out what she wanted to do. She found a program called the ILearn Project, for which she volunteered to teach English.

When I first found this opportunity, I was a little in doubt because I had never done anything like that and asked myself, "Can I really do this?" But when they accepted me into the program, I started teaching three girls, and I realized that I really liked teaching and that I was also learning while teaching. One of the best things from that experience was when one of the girls I was teaching applied to an online program in Japan that was being taught in English and got accepted; she sent me a wonderful message telling me how grateful she was for what I had taught her. The impact for me was that, in a way, I had changed one person's life, and that was the beginning for me. I knew I wanted to do more, and that is when I became active in Climate Science, a program which educates people about environmental issues and how important they are for the world's future. I became very involved in Climate Science and now organize events for their volunteers. I am also working on setting up a chapter of Girl Up to promote gender equality. We have already launched an Instagram campaign and a cultural competition to get girls involved in our events and programs.

I learned about Tilt Camp from an email. I applied and got accepted, and I worked with a group of four other people; we worked on developing a project called EducaAid to provide first aid education in schools because there is nothing like that here in Brazil. Tilt Camp gave me connections to other people, and networking with them has been very valuable. For example, I wanted to apply to a competition where you need to develop an app to solve some problem in the world, but to apply, you needed to be part of a team, not just do it as one person. So I put out a message to my network, something like, "Who likes technology and wants to help me form a team for this competition?" And I got a bunch of answers and was able to put together a team. I don't think that would have been possible for me to do two years ago, because I didn't have a network.

For me, I think the most difficult thing was in the beginning, when I knew I wanted to do something, but there wasn't anything through my school where I could find opportunities, where I could find what I wanted to do, so I just had to find something on my own. And that was hard, figuring out what I liked and what I did not want to do. But it got better as I did more, and now I know how to go about it.

I think that, as a young person, in the beginning you just want to change the world. Then, maybe as you get involved, you see that you cannot change the world. But you can have impact, and you can help someone or something in some way. I always think of the saying of Mother Teresa: "We feel that what we are doing is nothing but a drop in the ocean. But the ocean would be less without that one drop." I think that we can all do a little thing that makes a big difference. I think the most important thing is to be passionate about what you are doing, to find something that you are passionate about, so that when you talk about it, people will see the sparkle in your eyes.

JAMIE SGARRO: *OFFERING LGBTQ+ ASYLUM SEEKERS RESOURCES AND NETWORKING*

Cofounder, AsylumConnect (now InReach)

LGBTQ+ advocate and social entrepreneur Jamie Sgarro came relatively late to the nonprofit world. "It wasn't until I was in college that I even heard anything about social entrepreneurship or about working in nonprofit as being an actual career choice. I had never heard those terms and certainly never thought about making a living that way."

In college, Jamie met a fellow student named Sy, who had fled persecution in his home country as an LGBTQ+ asylum seeker. In their senior year of college, Jamie and Sy cofounded AsylumConnect,[9] the world's first resource website and app for people fleeing persecution and seeking asylum in the United States because of sexual orientation or gender identity. For Jamie and Sy, the cause was deeply personal. "I'm a big believer in drawing on personal experience," says Jamie.

When I think about how we started AsylumConnect—I have to laugh about it now—neither of us actually had engineering skills or a business background at that time, and here we were, running a tech nonprofit. But Sy had the personal experience of going through the LGBTQ+ asylum process and really seeing the gaps in coverage. I had the lived experience of coming from a conservative environment as a trans person, so it was really a case of just looking around and thinking—in your own life—what is the need that you know doesn't exist, and what would be the solution you would want to have? And I think that's the key: the most successful social impact organizations that I have seen are the ones that draw from the founder's personal experience.

When I think about people I admire who are running organizations based on their lived experience, I think about Aly Murray, cofounder and executive director of UPchieve, a nonprofit that uses technology to help low-income students achieve upward mobility. I had been running AsylumConnect for a couple of years, and she got in touch with me because she wanted to talk about starting a tech nonprofit. Since then, she's been extremely successful, and I think her success is because she really understands the issue area; she *was* that student she's now helping, and that personal experience gives her so much motivation. And that's essential because running a nonprofit is really hard, and it takes time and sacrifice, so you really need to be all in.

Unfortunately, something that I've seen occasionally is that young people starting out just went too fast, tried to scale too big, too soon, and didn't take the time to really think about what is the best growth strategy. For example, I've seen it happen that a new organization gets a big grant but didn't have the mentorship or structure to make use of it successfully, and it kind of slipped away, or else the solution wasn't what people really expected. So my best advice for young people starting out in this arena is to "start small, think big."

MAYA TIRONE-GOEHRING: *DEVELOPING A PASSION FOR CRIMINAL JUSTICE AND SOCIAL REFORM*

Volunteer and Activist for Criminal Justice Reform

For Maya Tirone-Goehring, the drive toward social activism started at a young age.

I think it started because I grew up in a very small, rural town: one stoplight, five churches, one gas station. Most of the people who went to my school were white, never left the town, never saw anyone who looked different from them. I would overhear the kind of things that people would say, which now I recognize as being very derogatory and discriminatory. I didn't understand what I was hearing, and I would go home and ask my parents, "What are they talking about? What are all these things, what does it all mean?" And it started to make me think, "That's not right, that can't be right," and that has been a trigger for me ever since I was very young. As I got older, in high school, we started a club called STOP—Students and

Teachers Opposed to Prejudice. It started off as a Gay-Straight Alliance, but we kind of moved it toward more social justice in general, and racial justice in particular, because we had some refugees enroll in our school, and people were not exactly gracious and accepting towards them. We also had a Mexican population that was not always treated the way they should be; for instance, the Mexican students were held back or put in special ed for not speaking English, instead of getting ESL (English as a Second Language) classes. So with STOP, we were actively asking the question, Why weren't we treating people equally? That inequality has always driven me to try to understand and figure out how to deal with its unfairness.

Maya's further journey into activism came in college, when she was able to travel to the southern border and Mexico with a group from school.

We were able to meet with Border Patrol and witnessed a deportation trial, which was a haunting experience. There was a huge mural of Donald Trump on the wall, and there was a judge, who spoke no Spanish but who was calling the young men on trial—who were only seventeen or eighteen years old—incompetent because they didn't speak English. Then we went into the mountains in Mexico, where we visited a women's cooperative, and we talked to the women about what they were experiencing, living with daily violence and fear of the drug cartels. This was all a shocking and eye-opening trip and made me determined to focus on how I can become more involved in social justice.

Since then, I've been able to work with local, young teens at an after-school center, many of them immigrants and living in rough neighborhoods, and heard their stories about being terrified of deportation and witnessing gun violence right where they lived. I also took a class in political science and religion at the Westchester County Jail alongside incarcerated people who had been accepted to attend my college when they are released from jail. Working with them opened my eyes to the concept of punishment and what that means to people, and that has inspired me to want to go into criminal justice reform.

I think the pandemic made people reevaluate how involved they can be. For instance, after the death of George Floyd, people were still quarantining. There were all these protests, but you had to think about whether or not you were going to go in person, or just show your support online—things that people never had to think about before. I think the pandemic has changed how some people think about activism; it's not always about marching or sit-ins or going to a demonstration. It has opened up many more avenues to inform people, engage people, and get young people involved. And we have to keep finding more ways to motivate people to confront injustice and work together to combat it.

I think a lot of young people think their voice doesn't matter. If it was made clearer to them that their voice *does* matter and that taking action in a movement or cause can actually make change happen, that would help. I think a lot of young people feel undervalued or underrepresented, and so they don't want to get involved. If volunteering or participating in activism was more valued—or even thought of as being as valuable as a job—I think more young people would take it on. But they need to be inspired; they have to feel that there is a wrong, and that they can help make it right.

These twelve young people came to activism from different backgrounds and perspectives and put their strengths to work on very different issues. But each of them brought to their work a determination and a conviction that they could improve or change a system that challenged them to make a difference. They each brought creativity, empathy, passion, and persistence to what they wanted to do—and each of them is continuing their pursuit toward finding ways to heal the world.

Chapter Three

Becoming an Activist

Changemaker, activist, social entrepreneur, advocate—these terms are sometimes used interchangeably, but the essence of the people they describe is the same: they are people who see a problem, think of ways to solve it, organize other people to help them, and lead actions to make a change in society. They are *influencers*, people who affect how others think or act. Successful activists get other people aligned with the cause they are working on and get them to work together to advance that cause in a positive way.

In 2018 *New York Times* writer David Brooks spoke with Bill Drayton, who, forty years ago, invented the term *social entrepreneur* and, among the other organizations he established, founded Ashoka, an organization which supports social entrepreneurship all over the world. Bill Drayton has been passionate about using social impact to make positive changes in the world. Bill Drayton's goal, Brooks writes, has been to make everyone a changemaker. "Changemakers," Brooks goes on to explain, are "people who can see the patterns around them, identify the problems in any situation, figure out ways to solve the problem, organize fluid teams, lead collective action and then continually adapt as situations change."[1]

What makes someone a changemaker, an activist? What I heard from so many of the people with whom I spoke is that what makes an activist is a sense of purpose. That sense of purpose comes from what's *in* them and what *matters* to them. It is that direct connection between a cause and the resonance it sounds in your heart. It is finding something that galvanizes you, that makes you want to *do something*, to fix something, to make something better. Becoming an activist means finding your purpose: what it is that really drives you, what gives you that feeling in your heart that something matters—and then chasing that feeling.

For many young people, what starts them on the road to activism is being confronted with something that hits them powerfully with the feeling, "That is *so* wrong!" It may be something in school, in the community, or somewhere else in the world that jolts you with the urge to do something. Whether it is finding out about contaminated ground water affecting the drinking water in your community, like it was for MC Hanafee LaPlante, or finding out that most people in your community don't have information about even rudimentary first aid, like it was for Kakooza Hakim learning about an issue in your community that is a problem is, for many young changemakers, the beginning of their journey. That sense of, "That bothers me and it continues to bother me, and instead of just turning my head away like everyone else seems to be doing, I'm going to chase it down and do something about it," is often the common thread in activism, no matter the issue.

This powerful feeling of wanting to right wrongs can start early. As Jessica Grose has written recently in the *New York Times* about her own young daughter's fierce urge toward action, "She's only 9, and anytime she learns something awful about the world she responds with outrage and a desire to change it, urgently. When she saw a magazine headline about the rapid decline of bee populations due to climate change, she earnestly explained, 'We need to save all the bees!'"[2]

"I want to bottle that energy and keep it with her, at least in some small way," continues Grose, "even as she becomes increasingly aware of the flawed world around her as she grows. She's a few years away from marching on the National Mall, but she's learning that progress doesn't happen without effort and determination."

In Katie Eder's view, there is often another element to why some young people become involved in a cause, and that is because they feel in some way socially isolated because of some difference, and that feeling drives a passionate desire to impact change. "If you think about it, in every high school across the country, there's some kids who feel like the odd one out, maybe a bit of a misfit. Maybe because they're queer, or Black, or Indigenous, or differently abled, they feel like an 'other,' and that's often the reason they become motivated to do something, to change something, because it directly affects them in some way, because they feel the inequity of it—for themselves and for others."

While you may already have some driving passion—some cause which has already gripped your interest and is inspiring you to take action—some young people just know they want to do *something*, but don't know where to turn to find some area in which to enlist their energy and determination. One excellent way to help you narrow down your interest is to take a look at the United Nations Seventeen Sustainable Development Goals (SDGs), which is a useful outline in which to begin to understand how critical issues facing the entire world are organized into areas of focus. These SDGs are listed with links in the resources section at the end of this book to learn more about them; the more you delve into them and expand your research, the more likely you will be to find a cause into which you want to throw yourself wholeheartedly.

But recognizing an injustice, an inequality, a deplorable or inhumane condition is just the first step; in and of itself, that doesn't make you an activist. If the first step on the road to activism is recognizing a wrong and wanting to do something about it, the second step is when that recognition leads—often immediately—to the question, "*What* can I do about it?" And when that question begins to percolate, to grow, and to turn into a fire in the belly or a passionate idea, that's what leads to activism.

There are many qualities which successful activists seem to share. Young changemakers I spoke with and adults in the field of social science and activism agreed on many of them and explained why these qualities matter and how they contribute to becoming an activist.

A SENSE OF PURPOSE

While the impulse to leap into activism can be instant, the process of becoming an activist usually doesn't happen overnight. Turning passion into action begins with purpose, and understanding what your purpose is. Knowing how and where you fit in is the beginning of understanding how you can make a difference. How do you get to that sense of purpose? One way to do it is to focus on thinking about what matters to *you* and why. If you don't look inside yourself and know your fire, you will be much less effective. Learn about what is happening in your community, your city, your country, and the world. Dig deeper into the issues that concern you; it's important to immerse yourself in learning about the issue that fuels your passion before you jump in and try to solve the problem. As you begin to understand yourself and the issues around you, you will see that your growing sense of purpose is shaped by everything you do and everything you experience.

Based on her own experience, Zoya Haq describes the early steps toward becoming an activist the following way:

> I think the first thing to do when you identify a flame that's igniting your fervor is to harness that emotion, then take advantage of it, don't let it go away. Talk it out with people that you know, talk about why you feel the way you do, and try and verbalize what it is that you're feeling. Why do you feel about it the way that you do? What do you want to see change? As you start to have those conversations with people in your circle, you'll realize a few things. First, they may give you back some ideas that expand your thinking; there may be some shared ideas that you can pull out of those conversations, even if they are not immediately visible. Second, once you start having those conversations, you start developing a more comprehensive understanding of whatever it is that you are trying to combat or that you're trying to overcome. And with that understanding comes more passion, and with that passion comes more understanding.

Having a sense of purpose—finding something that gives meaning to your life—is essential to activism. Laura Day, executive director of the Institute for Social Impact at the Hockaday School and a national leader in training young people to be involved in the world of social impact, explains:

> Starting with purpose is huge. When a young person feels that sense of purpose and can put a name to that feeling and connect it to what they do, then they chase that feeling because they want to keep feeling it. Finding the purpose that is meaningful to you makes all the difference. So, for example, if you volunteer to serve food at a food bank and you aren't particularly grabbed by the experience, then it's not for you. But if your heart responds to that experience and you connect with it, then it's meaningful and you want to get deeper into it.

Laura had a great way to articulate the process of finding that sense of purpose, of knowing exactly what you want to do and doing it: she talks about traffic and how you need to "find the lane you're meant to be in." Laura sees kids find their lane all the time—and, when they do, she says, "nothing can stop them." But first, they need to find the lane, then they need to understand what it is they want to do, and then they need a guide to help them accomplish their goals. Sometimes, she would say, kids just charge ahead. And when that happens, Laura has found she needs to stop them to help them look deeper into what they want to do. She might have inquired, for example, "Have you asked this? Have you been here? Do you know about that?" By stepping in and acting as a guide, she's helped young people deepen their understanding of their role and the action they want to pursue. "You have to take them back to the beginning," Laura says. "Ask the questions, make sure they understand what they want to do, why they want to do it, how they want to do it. Doing that helps them recognize, develop, and refine their sense of purpose."

EMPATHY

One quality which many consider a requisite of activism is empathy. What is empathy? The *Cambridge Dictionary* defines empathy as "the ability to share someone else's feelings or experiences by imagining what it would be like to be in that person's situation."[3]

That kind of sensitivity toward another person's situation, being able to see injustice or feel someone else's hunger or poverty, for example, is inherent in the drive to be a changemaker. And, as Laura Day explained, you need to have empathy and understanding before you launch into solving a social problem. To have empathy, Laura pointed out, you need to be able to notice things and be aware of how things affect other people. She has called it "widening the we"—finding ways to reach beyond ourselves, as well as reducing the kind of images and vocabulary which distances people and makes them seem "other." Laura encourages actively practicing empathy; for instance, try to visualize yourself in someone else's circumstances. One way to practice this is to actually select a random person on the street and think about what their life might be like. What kind of place do they live in? What kind of food do they eat? How do they spend their day? With whom do they live? What kind of aches or pains might they have? What are they worried about? Think about how you would feel, how you might act, and what you might need if you were living their life. A similar exercise is to read a news article about a person who is living in a war zone or dealing with homelessness or another difficult situation, and imagine their life, trying to feel what they must be going through. Get in the habit of doing that exercise occasionally; let it open your mind and your heart to other people's experiences. Practicing empathy can enable you to see people and their circumstances in greater context, as well as help you focus more clearly on problem solving.

RESILIENCE

Another key to becoming a successful activist is having resilience, the ability to try something and fail and try it again. To be able to look at what worked and what didn't and to go on to build on the things that worked—to persevere despite setbacks, rather than give up. Running away from failure, being deterred by something that didn't go according to plan is, as Russell Agustin puts it, "a losers' game."

As many of the young activists I spoke with expressed, you *will* make mistakes, although hopefully they will not be mistakes with significant consequences. Mistakes, they pointed out, are often how we learn something important, and so they can—and should—be considered as part of the learning process. In MC Hanafee LaPlante's words, "I think that all the mistakes I've made were part of the learning process. There were no mistakes that I made that were so awful that I wished I could go back and fix them. I really do think that I did everything I could with the knowledge that I had *in those moments* and that I made good, rational decisions. And I think that it worked out well for me. I feel very lucky to say it, but I don't think I would have changed anything."

MC continues, saying the following:

> People are going to tell you to be confident, to use your unique skills, or use your flaws, don't be scared, things like that. But I think that's just incredibly out of touch. Because if you're doing this work of activism, you're going to be scared, you're going to make mistakes, you're not going to know what you're doing, you're not going to know how to move forward. I think the most important thing that you can do if you're in that position is embrace it. Admit to yourself that you don't know what to do, then internalize that, and focus on what you need to be doing differently.

Recognize your flaws, but don't beat yourself up about them; work on them, and try to be OK about them. Know that they're not your strength, but still try to work to strengthen them. But also recognize your strengths, and work on them as well. Become the best that you can be, given who you are.

Being resilient enables you to make mistakes or even fail, but, despite that, to carry on. But when you do, the important thing is that you understand what happened, why it happened, why you made that mistake, and then figure out what to do right the next time. As Russell Agustin puts it, "Use failure as a tool to learn, and to succeed."

You may find that not everyone will admire or support what you are doing. In some communities or schools where there is no culture of activism or social entrepreneurship, you may find yourself faced with negative reactions, even ridicule, for the stance and actions you take. MC Hanafee LaPlante, for instance, found that her peers' reactions changed when she left the smaller, private middle school she had been at to attend a large public high school, where she became more involved in activism.

At first, there were a lot of undertones of, "Boy, she's so intense, why is she doing so much?" But that's kind of a normal response. But when I started doing the Period Rally work, talking about how even saying the word "period" was so stigmatized, I started feeling a shift in how I was viewed. A lot of the guys were like, "Ooooh, why are you doing that stuff? It's so gross!" And when I was actually interviewed on one of the biggest radio stations in Chicago about the rally, there was a lot of backlash at school, a lot of gossip like, "Oh, she actually said that? How could she talk about that on the radio? She's so weird!" It was really disheartening to get those reactions, especially because the whole point of the rally was to stop that kind of thing from happening. But it also solidified our need for the rally, because it proved that the issue existed and that we needed to change the way people think. But it was definitely an uncomfortable few weeks at school for me. Then when the story got picked up by PBS and the *Chicago Tribune* and became more openly mainstream, suddenly people were like, "OMG, it's so cool what you're doing!" I have to say, though, that getting to that point was definitely not a fun experience.

SELF-CONFIDENCE

Being an activist takes a certain self-confidence, self-reliance, and a kind of moral compass, an innate sense of right and wrong. For Hayat Hassan, it was a determination not to take anything as fact which drove her. "I've always been outspoken," Hayat told me.

> Even my fourth grade teacher told me I should become a lawyer because I would always try to rebut everything I was told. I've always actually found joy in trying to find alternatives or trying to disprove certain things that we were told to take as fact. Even back in fourth grade history class, I would read the textbook with the aim of trying to find things to contradict; I would do my own personal research just to find contradictions. Even though that in itself is not a form of activism, I've always been interested in turning on its head things we take as fact, disproving things that we are told to accept, and always being very conscious of what I am accepting, what I am believing—in a sense, building my own moral compass.

From Zoya Haq's perspective, being a very young activist taught her a valuable lesson. Zoya explained the following:

> The hardest part, I think, of being a young activist is that it's easy to feel a sense of imposter syndrome at any stage of the process. When I started doing this, and I started when I was thirteen, I remember thinking, "How can I do this? I'm not going to be able to make any kind of difference because I'm so young." And that feeling kind of follows you throughout the journey because even as you get older, you'll be working with people who are older and older, and you always feel a little bit out of place, a little like an outsider. But then you realize that, no matter what, if you're making even a little bit of impact, you deserve to be wherever you are.

It takes courage to stand up for your beliefs, it takes confidence to try to persuade others to share them, and it takes a kind of fierce independence to work for—or against—an issue that you are passionate about. It takes self-reliance because you may be starting your journey on your own, before you find colleagues or supporters to join you. You may find these qualities within yourself already, but if you don't feel they are your strong points now, you can practice them and learn to develop them. As one young person has suggested only half-jokingly, "Fake it till you make it."

ADAPTABILITY

João Pedro talks about the importance of being able to face obstacles and pivot when necessary to make changes that might take your work in another direction.

When we were at Tilt Camp, we didn't have a lot of time to develop our project. Some of the group I was working with were in their senior year of high school, and their schoolwork didn't give them a lot of time to work on the project. We had to create a website, create social media, and create our plan, and all that took a lot of work. And then we also had to constantly change our idea to improve it, and we were constantly getting feedback and trying not to get too down from hearing things that weren't always positive and just learn from them. At one point, we had worked a lot on the idea that we were going to just donate computers, and the people at Tilt Camp told us to consider finding a better way to accomplish what we wanted to do—increase access to technology for underprivileged students—and we were so disheartened that we thought of giving up and trying again the next year. But then the leaders at Tilt Camp told us, "You have this opportunity now, don't leave it for later," so we really just had to put in a lot of work—a lot of hours working—because we were down to the wire, preparing our pitch and writing text that we would submit to the judges, and we had to listen to feedback and try to make our idea better. It wasn't easy, but I'm very happy that I did. I know it was good for me, and I know it was good for the other people on my team too.

A *pitch*—as in "to pitch your idea" or "make a pitch"—means to present your idea to try to persuade someone to support your idea or project. In order to be successful, a good pitch should be well thought out, organized carefully, with appropriate backup information or material, succinct, and well rehearsed.

AWARENESS OF THE WORLD BEYOND YOUR CAUSE

While you may be captivated by a very specific issue, whether it is climate change or racial justice, education equity, or anything else, it is important to keep yourself informed and engaged by what else is going on in the world. Activism does not happen in a vacuum; change movements do not take place in separate silos, each of which stands alone. Being an informed citizen will leave you better able to relate your cause to the larger picture of what is going on around you.

It is important to understand the global context of whatever issue concerns you—how the issue you are focused on relates to other issues in the world. If your passion is to ensure that no family in your community goes hungry, you need to think about—and learn about—food insecurity and how that relates to poverty, unemployment, housing, access to healthcare, nutritional awareness, and other social problems locally, nationally, and globally. Learn what organizations that focus on any of these issues may be doing that connects to your area of interest. The more you become informed about related issues, the better informed you will be about your own area of focus.

Being informed about world events also opens your mind—and your heart—to everything that goes on around you, beyond your neighborhood, beyond your community. None of us exist in isolation; we are all connected in humanity, and the problems that confront one group will inevitably impact others. Similarly, solutions that can allay one problem may be able to be applied to solve another, so being aware of what others are doing can be an important source of inspiration and motivation.

From realizing a sense of purpose to developing empathy, from building resilience and recognizing the value of learning from mistakes to understanding your place in the world and how world events affect the cause which drives you, these qualities will help shape your success in activism. Jonah Docter-Loeb eloquently sums up what he thought an activist should be:

> What I want out of an activist, a changemaker, and what I'm striving to be is someone who is very thoughtful and deliberate about what they do and why they do it. Someone who is constantly thinking, "Here is something I can do to make a difference," but also, "Is this the best way of doing it? Am I tackling the root cause, am I going about this in a way that won't have *negative* impact? Am I actually talking to the people being affected

by this issue?" And I think it's really important to be authentic, be who you really are, and don't try to fit into the mold of what you think a youth activist should be doing based on anything you've seen others do. And those are things I'm trying to do every day, knowing that I always have room for improvement. But I want someone—and I want to be that person—who has those types of qualities.

While these qualities may not all be part of every changemaker, together they show the range of the strengths, the inherent gifts, and the acquired skills which can help guide and support anyone on their path to creating positive change in the world. It is not enough to be outraged by injustice or inhumanity; it is important to recognize that every one of us has the ability to take action to make a positive difference. It is important to consider this when embarking on your journey in social activism: look inside yourself first, then zoom out to put yourself in the bigger picture. Find yourself, learn about yourself. Work from the inside out. In activism, if there's no inside, your outside is just anger yelling.

Chapter Four

Three Fundamentals of Activism

There are many components that go into making social change happen effectively, and they rarely come together quickly or without a lot of planning and hard work. In a later section, we will take a look at some of the tools you can learn to use to accomplish your goals, but first, there are three fundamental components to successful changemaking which you should understand and work on putting into practice as you set out on your journey. These three fundamentals are (1) understanding your cause, (2) motivating people to become involved, and (3) organizing for action. These basic building blocks to being an effective changemaker mean, first, that you will really understand the issue that you want to change; second, that you will know how to involve other people in supporting that change and helping you achieve what you want to do; and third, that when you do get them involved, you will know how to organize them to work together for maximum impact. Fully understanding your issue and learning how to motivate people and organize them to work together may be the most important steps in your growth as an activist.

UNDERSTANDING YOUR CAUSE

It is very easy to be captivated by a cause; you read something, you see something, or you hear something that activates your sense of injustice or empathy or ignites your outrage. When you find yourself drawn to action, to making change, to working to make something better, it's natural to just want to jump right in—join a march, sign a petition, or post a tweet. But being impulsive, being uninformed, is usually not the best way to become involved. Before you throw yourself wholeheartedly into action to support a cause, make sure you understand not only what it is about but also who the people involved in it are. There are several reasons why this is an important step. Perhaps the most important reason is to make sure that what you get involved with is authentic; with the instantaneous and explosive reach of the internet and social media, there are legions of clever hoaxes and outright criminal malefactors working to take advantage of people who want to do good. It is also important to understand your cause so that you can explain it to others, whether it is for the purpose of engaging their help, soliciting their funds, or motivating them to join you in your actions. It is very easy to become involved in an activity you don't really understand out of good faith and youthful innocence. I learned this from personal experience: When I was about fourteen years old, a school friend asked me to help her stuff envelopes for her mother's election campaign for local government. I thought it would be a fun thing to do, and we spent a pleasant afternoon in the campaign office readying flyers for mailing. It was only after I got home and told my parents about my afternoon's activity that they explained that my friend's mother was running on a campaign platform which was contrary to their beliefs, beliefs which I shared. I realized how even something as innocent as helping a friend stuff flyers into envelopes was, in fact, working *against* something I believed in; it was then that I promised myself I would look carefully into any cause I was tempted to support and make sure I understood what it was about.

So before you throw yourself into action, do your homework; there are lots of causes and organizations doing good work on issues that may grab you. If you hear about something that engages your interest and focus, spend some time learning more about it. Do your research online, in the library, and by talking with others. Look for organizations near you that are supporting the cause that interests you, and attend a meeting or talk with someone from the organization about what they are doing and how you may be able to fit in. The more you learn, the more prepared you will be to work effectively.

Zoya Haq had an excellent way to describe how passion for a cause can lead to greater understanding and how those forces thrive on each other. She used the image of a ladder that you climb: As you develop passion for a cause, you begin to talk about it with people. As you talk about it, you share ideas and gain further understanding; that understanding can lead to even greater passion. But, Zoya explained, it's very important as you harness the emotion which is driving you that you also do your research and start trying to learn more about the root of the problem you are passionate about. Find out why it is happening; find out whom in your community you can ask about it and who in your community might be able to help you address it.

As Zoya pointed out, we all have the internet at our fingertips, and almost everything is accessible online. In Zoya's experience, doing research, finding people to approach, and reaching out to them was key. "Some of my most meaningful opportunities," Zoya told me, "have come about when I get angry about an issue and think to myself, 'Who am I going to find who might be able to do something about it?' Then I look them up and get their contact information, and I'll send out blind emails to them, or blind messages to them, and one of them is going to hit, one of them is going to respond if you send out enough. And I think that's key to getting started."

Before launching yourself into action on an issue that you are passionate about, take some time to step back and learn more thoroughly about the issue, who is working in that arena, and what they are doing about it. Jamie Sgarro talked about why that step is valuable:

> I'd advise young people who want to become changemakers to first look around, explore whether there may already be solutions for the issue you want to address. Make sure that your solutions are not redundant; it may not make sense for you to put all your energy and resources into starting a new organization if there are others doing very similar work. It might make more sense for you to join an existing organization and just work to make that better. I've had young people call me and ask if they could talk with me about their idea. I'm not an issue expert in all those fields, so sometimes my advice may not be as helpful as other times, but it is important that they reach out for information, for background that will help them understand things more fully.

An enormous—and sometimes overwhelming—amount of material is available online. One of the most valuable skills you can learn is how to do online research, and, of course, there is a lot of online information about *how* to do online research. However, understand that some of that information is geared toward academic and scientific research and may be less relevant to the type of research you may want to do. Also, keep in mind that not all online information is useful or reliable. Learn how to be a discerning user of the internet—how to look things up quickly, how to sort through relevant and irrelevant sites and not fall down a rabbit hole or get diverted away from your primary focus. Doing research can be endlessly fascinating, enormously rewarding, and extremely useful; the more facile and experienced you become at doing research, the more likely you are to find valuable information quickly and efficiently.

Putting understanding into action becomes a powerful way to live your beliefs. The more you know about what you care about, the more likely you will be to strengthen your sense of purpose and deepen your involvement. In essence, let your actions demonstrate your seriousness, your commitment, and your understanding of the cause you are fighting for.

MOTIVATING PEOPLE

You know that you are passionate about a cause, that there is a problem that you are driven to want to help fix. So how do you get other people to care about it as much as you do and to join you in action with the same energy and enthusiasm that you have? Elsewhere in this section, we will explore the power of organization, how a group of people working together is infinitely more effective than just one person working alone. But first you need to address the following questions: How do you get people to become energized and motivated enough to work together with passion and mutual respect? How do you inspire them with that "feeling of enthusiasm you get from someone or something that gives you new or creative ideas," that makes you want to do or achieve something?[1] How do you get them to feel that same fire, that same sense of purpose that you do?

There are lots of ways to inspire people, and there are many tools to help you do that which you can add to your toolbox. Looking at the history of activism and learning from experienced activists will offer ideas about tools that have been used in the past to motivate people to join social action movements. Let's take a look at some that have proven to be very effective.

Storytelling

Throughout history people have loved telling stories and listening to stories. Telling a vivid story, particularly a story with a personal connection, can be a potent way to catch people's attention and engage their emotions. Being able to tell your own story, the story of how and why you are involved in something, can be singularly powerful. Marshall Ganz, a professor at Harvard University and an influential trainer and organizer for political campaigns and other groups, explains the power of what he calls leadership storytelling:

> A leadership story is first a story of self, a story of why I've been called. . . . You have to claim authorship of your story and learn to tell it to others so they can understand the values that move you to act, because it might move them to act as well.[2]

Katie Eder shares her thoughts on why storytelling can be so important in motivating people to become involved. To Katie, storytelling is a motivating force not just because people want to hear someone's personal story, but because it allows people to see themselves as part of a bigger picture.

> When we look back in history to moments when people have been mobilized in large numbers to take collective action, there was always a sense of "I am part of something bigger" and a sense of very clear purpose. I think the way to get people to feel that sense of purpose is by what I call inspiration empowerment. Inspiration empowerment comes from telling stories of other people, people who are taking action and being a part of collective action. Those stories have power and can inspire young people and make them realize that sense of purpose, the sense that we all want to work together. I think that's how it begins, and when it is powerful and effective, then people are inspired. And when they're inspired, then there's the possibility of their becoming deeply engaged.

Jamie Sgarro echoed the value of storytelling, particularly when the person sharing their story is another young person, someone whose story will resonate and whom teens might relate to and be moved to emulate.

Peer-to-peer connection can be an important motivator, especially when the person telling their story is someone teens can relate to. "What's the best way to make an impact on young people?" Jamie asks rhetorically, "Bring young voices in, cool people whose stories will inspire them."

Learning to be able to tell your own story—the story of why you became passionately involved in your cause and what it means in your life—may not come easily. But as you begin to talk to people, as you get asked why you became involved, work on refining what you want to say. Think about what the most relevant points in your story are, what the most interesting or surprising or emotional things about your personal journey are, and develop them into a narrative that has a framework—a beginning, a middle, and a present or future. When you tell it to people, listen to the questions they ask, and then anticipate them and weave the answers into your story. What you should aim for is to fine-tune your narrative and make it more focused so that you are able to tell it—again and again—fluently and eloquently, without it sounding rote or scripted. A good storyteller can tell a story again and again, with each listener feeling as though they are hearing someone tell it for the first time.

Using Music to Bring People Together

Throughout human history music has been a means to motivate people: religious music has guided and brought people together in worship, rhythmic drumming and martial music have emboldened and impassioned people to warfare, and folk and popular music have galvanized and unified people in antiwar demonstrations and labor movements. We talk about how music moves us because music taps directly into our emotions and our physical being. Music connects and engages people in a very basic, visceral way, and it has been used as a force for action and change for generations.

In an article in *Africa Renewal*, Dana Da Silva writes, "The combination of the right lyrics, rhythm and instruments can build a group identity, stir strong emotions, engage audiences and amass people to take action. This makes it the perfect partner for social change."[3] As Tracey Nicholls writes, "It is because of the way music feeds into our emotional lives and because of the sense of social well-being we get from sharing emotional states with others that music so frequently accompanies movements that build, and depend upon, solidarity."[4]

The power of music to be a motivating force in action is not just that it can spark emotions and draw people together, but that its power lingers in the mind and is reinforced through repetition. As Joe Hill—songwriter, poet, public speaker, and organizer for the Industrial Workers of the World labor union—wrote in 1914, "A pamphlet, no matter how good, is never read more than once, but a song is learned by heart and repeated over and over."[5]

Today, as throughout history, music continues to be an effective motivator: from call-and-response chants during protest marches to hip-hop and rap artists proclaiming against social injustice, racism, and police brutality, music engages and empowers people with a gripping combination of rhythm, melody, and message, which can make people leap to their feet with an urge to act. And using music to stir people to action is not just the territory of adults: witness the young teen drumming prodigy, Nandi Bushell, raising passion and action for climate change through music. Her song "The Children Will Rise Up,"[6] recorded with her friend Roman Morello, has become an anthem for environmental action with its powerful beat and urgently compelling lyrics. Even President Barack Obama posted her video on his Facebook page, writing, "Many social movements have been started and sustained by young people. Nandi and Roman used music as a way to share their compelling message about why we need to take action on climate change."[7] Recognition doesn't come any bigger than that!

Music isn't just a unifier, it can be an enticement: if you are planning a meeting, a rally, or a fundraising event, if you are able to get a great DJ or a lively band to play—and you are able to announce it beforehand—that can certainly go a long way in bringing people to the event. Even without doing that, plan to have recorded music playing while your attendees are gathering. It's not only a good background as people mingle or find seats, but hearing a good beat or a great sound, other people are likely to stop in their tracks or wander over just to listen—and if you're prepared to welcome them in, you may just find yourself with new recruits.

Help People Feel Useful

Most people want to feel useful and that they are doing something meaningful, but sometimes people just don't know how or where they can fit in. By showing them concrete and worthwhile ways that they can become involved in your work, you are helping them to feel useful and included in action. Katie Eder says the following:

> There's a space for everybody in any kind of organizing or changemaking. No matter what your skill is, whether it's drawing or writing or speaking, building relationships, or driving, there's always a place where someone's talents can be used. You sometimes have to be creative about putting someone to work and making sure they know they are needed. Even if it's doing something physical—like carrying large objects!—you are getting someone involved in something meaningful they can do, something that needs to be done. Believe me, there always seems to be something heavy that needs to be moved!
>
> I like to tell people there's a role for everybody in activism; people shouldn't have to feel that you need to be a certain kind of activist. You can be whoever you are, do whatever you feel you want to do, and you can find a place in a movement or an issue that matters to you.

Putting people to work, though, is just one part of using people effectively. You need to make sure that the people who help you and who join you in action feel valued and appreciated and that you are thoughtful about how you use their time. One of the most important lessons that Jonah Docter-Loeb has learned about motivating volunteers is to think carefully before assigning tasks. "It's important to know what you need someone to do and how to be able to explain how it needs to be done. I know there were times when I made things overly complicated or when I assigned tasks that were more my own passion projects or side projects than they were actual tasks that needed doing," Jonah reflects. "I realize now that I wasn't really respecting peoples' time, and I learned that that's a clear path to frustrating volunteers or even losing their interest or willingness to work."

The last thing you want to do is lose your hard-won supporters, especially when you've put so much effort into recruiting them. So be thoughtful and strategic in planning what you want people to do and how you will engage their time and talents in ways that will ensure that they feel included and valued.

Build Community

People are more inclined to work together when they feel connected to others; building those relationships, building that sense of community, is an important step in motivating people. Katie Eder points out the following:

> One thing that I found is so crucial is being able to feel that you are part of a community of young people who are doing something important together. And that's why, when people tell me they want to get involved, my recommendation is always to first get involved locally because when you're in your community, working with people locally, that's where change begins to happen—but it's also where the fun begins to happen. And the best parts of organizing, the best parts of revolutions, happen on the ground, locally—when you're building those relationships, building that sense of community, and honing that sense of purpose.
>
> Relationship building is a priority when it comes to motivating people. Relationships are the foundation of everything; building relationships, building trust, building community, those are the most important things. When you are doing something together, you're just so much stronger, even if it takes a little more time to get buy-in from different people, different stakeholders, than it might by trying to do something yourself. And when you're able to get those people to really work together, that's just so much more powerful, so much more effective. It's easy to try to do things alone, and early on in my time as an organizer, I put a lot of pressure on myself because I felt like the whole thing was on me. But now I know I would never want to do a project or organize something by myself; I'd never do that again. I've really learned that you have to lean on the people around you, trust people, and build those relationships so that you can divide the work and divide the pressure and the responsibility—but then you also get to share the excitement, the good parts, with other people. And that's just so, so critical.

What is a *stakeholder*? A stakeholder is someone who has a stake—an interest—in a particular enterprise; it is someone who is involved or affected by a course of action.

Relational Organizing

Relational organizing means mobilizing people within your own network—community, school, or social—to engage with the cause you are working for. As an article on the NAACP website points out, "It's not exactly a new term, in fact, it's used to describe something you do all the time: talking to people you know personally and persuading them to take an action on something."[8] It is probably the most effective means to engage people because it *is* personal. If people know you and trust you, they are more likely to listen to what you say. Peer-to-peer organizing, or relational organizing, can be absolutely essential in furthering support for your cause. Going to your neighbors, talking with your friends or with your family, ensuring that they are informed about the issues, and understanding why you are working on a cause is using your own power to build the organization and mobilize action within your circle.

Micro-Influencers

For Wisdom Cole, the power of what he calls *micro-influencers* is vital to the success of an organization and a movement. Micro-influencers are those people in the community who are constantly engaging with others, talking with people, and interacting within the community. These are people like the barber, the librarian, or the mail carrier; these key people within the neighborhood and the community can be very effective in influencing a local network of people because they are well known, trusted, and seen within the community every day. The impact that they can have in promoting a message can be essential to a local organization. So identifying those micro-influencers and engaging their interest in your cause can help to move other people in the community into your sphere.

Reaching People beyond Your Own Network

Wisdom Cole describes ingenious ways people mobilized others to register to vote in the last election. In one case, when a local Popeye's restaurant announced a new chicken sandwich, people lined up around the block to get an early taste, and savvy volunteers quickly showed up to register people to vote while they were waiting in line. It is that ability to meet people where they are which can be a great way to reach new contacts. A senior center, a community recreation area, or even a line for a movie or restaurant can present opportunities to engage with new people.

Wisdom said the following on the topic:

> You need to start with things on a local scale. It's about making sure, for example, that there are local election wins that people are seeing. Working locally can be so important. Often people think that they need to come to Washington, DC, to fight at the federal level, to be part of a movement, but there are things that are happening in your locality that you can be part of, and it's those local wins that inform national narratives.
>
> When you can develop relationships with locally elected officials, people who understand how their system works, then we are able to see America in a better picture. Your mayor, your city council—these are the key people you have to develop relationships with. Organizing, building power, is about relationships—relationships with your officials, relationships with other organizations, other local people who are actually being affected by the thing you are fighting for.

ORGANIZING FOR ACTION

A single person can launch a protest; they can march, they can raise their voice, and they can demonstrate against something that moves them to action. But a single person is just one voice, one actor. Think how much further their impact will be felt if they are not alone; if they were joined by hundreds, thousands of others; if their voice was echoed and magnified by hundreds of voices; and if they were not marching alone but marching with throngs of others united by a single vision. Think of how Greta Thunberg began her protest against climate change with a solo, silent protest as she held up a sign reading "School strike for climate" outside the Swedish Parliament in 2018.[9] That protest started with a single individual making a personal statement. It was when thousands of students around the world began to join her protest by participating in school strikes against climate change that her effectiveness was magnified. That is the power of organizing: to amplify the message and ensure the mobilization of many others behind a single cause.

Writing in the *New York Times*, Robin Marty has described the power of organized action succinctly:

With so many systems in place to tap into already, the issue isn't so much finding a way to help—it's about maximizing impact. One person calling a local lawmaker 200 times might be considered harassment. But 200 people calling that legislator once is impossible to ignore. Likewise, a single $100 donation does immediate good, but a recurring $10 donation—especially if a friend or 20 will join you—can provide ongoing funding that an organization can rely on. One national march of a million people makes headlines for a time. But small, ongoing actions . . . are tactics that grow more powerful the longer they last.[10]

Social and political movements gain traction and build power when people organize to work together; such organization is not a new concept. "The United States has a long history of people organizing for social change. Early organization for change came from labor protests, which originated as early as colonial times (Mises Institute, 2009). The first recorded strike for higher wages occurred in Philadelphia in 1786, and was initiated by shoe makers (2009). Perhaps more famously, workers organized to strike in the industrial revolution, leading to the types of unions we are more familiar with today."[11]

There are other benefits of organization beyond the sheer number of people involved. When action is taken as a group, people can take on different roles, using their individual skills where they are most needed. Organization offers mutual support—working together with others who care about the same things you do—drawing you into a circle of people with similar ideals and goals; you share the excitement, you share the work, you share the successes, and you may share failure. But you are not alone.

For most people who want to be involved in activism, joining an existing organization is the simplest, most straightforward way to participate. If you are motivated by the passion to become involved in a social action project, the first thing that makes sense to do is to find other people who feel the same way you do and are already involved in working in that movement. It is very likely that you will find others who are already doing something about the issue that is galvanizing you. How do you begin to find that collective? "You can start," Wisdom Cole has suggested, "by thinking about what organizations are doing things in your neighborhood, in your state, in your city, that you can be a part of, that can be part of transformational change." Keep your eyes and ears open at school, within your community, and at local media outlets to find out who else might be involved and what they are doing. Go to an exploratory meeting or to the next activity that may be posted and see how you might become more involved and how you can join.

"It's essential to join an organization," Wisdom Cole said. "When we're thinking about the longevity of a movement, it's really about being a part of an organization and developing collective power." Wisdom explains further: "Going to a protest once or our posting something one time, that can be good, but it's not necessarily sustainable. Strength comes from making sure that you are part of a collective, a group of people that's constantly pushing for collective change."

Noted activist and organizer Heather Booth eloquently describes the power and importance of organizing from her own personal experience:

> I think young people, all people, need to know that *if* we organize, *if* we take action, *we can change the world.* Young people *have* changed the world, even when it seemed impossible. But it needed taking action and joining with others—and that's the act of organizing.
>
> I have seen this happen when I was in Mississippi in 1964: During the civil rights movement, there was a national project called Freedom Summer, and Northern college students were recruited to go down South and support Black people in Mississippi who were being terrorized. This project gained national notoriety when three young volunteers, Andrew Goodman, James Chaney, and Michael Schwermer, were killed at the hands of the Ku Klux Klan. At that point it seemed hopeless: no matter what you did, you couldn't win. But because people organized, because they took action, within a year there was a voting rights act.

Heather goes on to describe why organizing for action is not just about promoting a cause but about bringing people together with respect and caring.

> In that early movement, we talked about building a beloved community. A community where we treated each other with dignity and respect and caring. We supported each other, and we had a vision of what we'd like to see in the society we were building.
>
> The big lesson, I think, is that if we want to make things better in this world, whether it's in the environment or ensuring that people have healthcare or that we have the services we need or that you can afford school education, that all these things can happen—but only if we organize. And that the way in which we should organize is to build a caring society with love at the center. We don't need to be alone; we can find

others, we can build organization, we can build bonds of friendship, and with that, we can learn together—not to be perfect but to *try* together, and through our trying, learn both from our successes and even from our failures, as long as we're in it together.

If you haven't found a local group working on the issue that is igniting your passion, then it may be time for *you* to be the one doing the organizing. This was the route that some of the young changemakers I spoke with for this book chose: whether they started alone or with one or two peers as they began their projects, they soon recognized that they needed to bring other people in to join them in their efforts. But how do you begin to organize? How do you find the people to work with you?

If organizing is about bringing people together, the first step in doing that is meeting people and talking with them about the issue which concerns you. You can start in the most local way possible: talk with your friends, talk with your family, and talk with your neighbors. Talking with people doesn't just spread the word or engage their interest; as you talk with them about the issue you have identified, you will begin to focus your thoughts about it and refine your message. From that first small circle of people, you will want to reach out further; first to the friends-of-friends circle and then expanding outward into the community. At this point, you will probably want to set up a meeting to begin to organize into a working group. You will need to think about how many people you might gather and where you will meet. Will it be in someone's home, in a classroom at school, or in a community center? Although in the past few years we have grown accustomed to virtual meetings, it is much more effective for people to meet face to face when possible, so think about how you will start engaging people in what you want to do.

How will you let people know about your meeting? Will you prepare flyers and distribute them, and will you post them in public spaces? Will you leave them on a table? Think about where people might see them; local supermarkets, libraries, and recreation centers often have a community bulletin board where such information can be posted. Some public spaces—and even some private spaces, such as doctors' waiting rooms or barber shops—have a table where materials can be left. Keep in mind, though, that there may be rules about where or what kind of flyers may be posted or how they might be distributed. Ask whether

Tabling refers to the practice of setting up a table with your organization's flyers, information, or petitions in a location where you or your team have the opportunity to tell people about your work or the issue in which you are involved. There are often invited opportunities to set up a table at a community event, school fair, or organizational event. Tabling can also refer to setting up a table anywhere you might find people to engage. It is important to make sure that setting up a table does not interfere with pedestrian or vehicular traffic, as well as ensuring that it is permissible. If you or one of your team will be on hand at the tabling event, make sure you are prepared to answer questions or take down contact information so that you can get back to people with more information or add names to your mailing list.

posting or leaving materials is permitted; you don't want to run the risk of annoying or antagonizing anyone, let alone getting into trouble, especially not just when you are getting started.

These days, social media is an excellent way to alert people to something you are doing. Think carefully, though, about how you will restrict access to what you post so that you have people who are genuinely interested in the meeting or event attend, without encouraging unwanted or unscrupulous attendees.

Organizing is about building relationships—relationships with the people who will work with you on moving forward toward achieving your goals, relationships with your constituents (the people who are affected by the issue you have identified), and relationships with the people who hold the power to carry out the changes you want to see happen, such as people in office, legislators, and community leaders. As you begin forming your organization, you are also working on building those relationships. The best way to start this process is to start small, start local; these are the key relationships which will be your base and hopefully will help you expand to an ever-growing community of support and action.

Elsewhere in this book, we explore ways to motivate people once you have begun to reach out to them, as well as tools that you can use as you develop your efforts in activism and advocacy. But as you start to build your community—the people who will be involved in your movement, your action—keep in mind the goal of educating them, informing them, and bringing them together for a unifying cause. This is a responsibility, but when you carry it out with honesty, with integrity, and with the best intentions to do good, you will find that it resonates within you and beyond you and will help make your journey more meaningful and more effective.

I turned to one of the nation's leading organizational strategists, Heather Booth, about what teens should think about when they are becoming involved in social activism and working toward positive change. Heather Booth has been training people in how to organize for decades; almost fifty years ago, she founded Midwest Academy, a national training institute committed to advancing the struggle for social, economic, and racial justice. Since its founding, Midwest Academy has trained thousands of grassroots activists in an organizing philosophy, methods, and skills to actively participate in the democratic process.[12] Although Midwest Academy does not have a program for teen activists, Heather talked with me about what young activists should know about organizing. Heather has explained the following:

There are specific skills that one can learn for successful protest and activism—practical things such as: How do you hold a meeting? How do you hold people's attention? How do you speak effectively in public? How do you raise funds? How do you get publicity? How do you build a loving community?

But there are also strategic talents that can be learned. You need to learn strategy, which means making a plan for how you get from where you start to where you want to go. You don't usually win with just one event or just one tactic; it is usually not enough to say, "Let's start a Twitter storm," or, "Let's march on the Capitol," or, "Let's stage a sit-in." Those may be good ideas—or they may not be —but they are not a

Grassroots, when used in the context of an activist or social impact movement, usually refers to organizing or starting at the most basic level—for instance, within a neighborhood or a local community.

strategy. You need a strategy, a long-term plan, in order for your movement to be successful. A strategy should have structure, and it should ask at least five questions. Answering those questions, developing your plan based on those questions, creates a strategy. Those questions can be learned, and they can be put to use.

FIVE QUESTIONS FOR BUILDING A STRATEGY

What Do You Really Want to Accomplish?

As Heather Booth points out, you need to think hard about what it is that you actually want to accomplish, as well as how you can tell when you have accomplished that goal. You need to be able to identify your goal: Is your goal to have your community stop spraying pesticides near a children's playground? Is your goal to have your school designate an all-gender restroom? Is your goal to start a tutoring service for underserved youth? Once you formulate your goal, then you need to figure out how you will know when you have reached that goal; you need to establish a measure of achievement. The measure of achievement may be that pesticides will no longer be sprayed within one thousand feet of one playground, or it may be that no pesticides will be sprayed near any playground in your town. Or the measure of achievement may be that one all-gender restroom will be designated in your school, or it may be that every school in your community will have an all-gender restroom. Or a measurement of success may be enrolling twenty middle school children in a twice-a-week tutoring program and completing one semester of tutoring. These are measurable goals: they are either successful or they are not. They may be partially successful—perhaps only five children will be enrolled in the tutoring program, for example—in which case, you then evaluate what worked and what didn't and can then plan to incorporate the improvements into the next stage of fulfilling your goal.

Who Has the Power to Grant You What You Want?

The answer to this question will determine the person who holds the key to fulfilling your goal, the person you must ultimately persuade to support your project. That is often a specific person—for example, the principal of your school or the mayor of your town. It is sometimes, though, an administrative body—for example, the board of education or the town council. You need to think about which individual or which administration holds the power to grant your request. If you are working toward eliminating pesticides near local parks, it may be the town council. If you are working toward getting an all-gender restroom in your school, it may be the principal or it may be the board of education. But in building your strategy, you will be planning the steps to persuade that ultimate person/administration to support your goal and enable you to succeed.

Who Is the Constituency, and How Do You Build Its Power?

The third question you need to answer is, Who is your constituency? Who are the people you are working to help? Who are the people who will benefit from your success? Also, who are the people who will work with you toward fulfilling your goal?

If you are working to reduce pesticide spraying near playgrounds, your constituency includes the children and young adults who use the playground, as well as their parents, who want to ensure the safety and health of their families. It may also be local neighbors, even if they don't have children, because ground contamination by pesticides can affect their drinking water as well as, perhaps, the value of their property. It may also include local dog walkers, whose pets frequent the parks and may be exposed to unhealthy substances. Thinking through all the possible people affected by the issue you have identified will help you determine to whom you will reach out and even how to reach out in the best way possible.

Identifying your constituents is your first step in building your community and developing your network; that will be how you develop your power. As Heather Booth points out, you need to know for whom you are working and with whom you are working. It's not enough to try to launch a movement because you are morally right; you need to identify your allies, your core group of people who will come together to build the power of the movement, so that it's not just one person standing up and shaking their fist, it's many people—tens, hundreds, and even thousands of people—working together toward a common goal.

How Do You Build Organizational Strength?

Heather's fourth question deals with the day-to-day practicalities of organizing, the very specific things you need to build your organization. In order to build an organization, it is usually important to have a leader, someone who will be the primary driver propelling the project forward, but you also need to develop other leaders, people who will be able to take on other leadership roles and work closely together to ensure that plans are carried out with coordination and effectiveness. This is also important because sometimes people resign from an organization even if they founded it, or they will give up a leadership role; for example, some of the young people highlighted in this book who started organizations while they were in high school found that leaving for college meant giving up their active leadership role because of time constraints, even if they remain active and involved. Ensuring that there is more than one person who has the knowledge and capacity to lead gives a sustainability to the organization it might not have if it were dependent on one person alone.

You also build organizational strength through raising money, and you build organizational strength through getting publicity and attention for your cause, your meetings, and your events. As you build your organizational strength, you will find yourself dealing with what seem like smaller questions like: Do we need to rent a meeting room? Do we need to pay to print flyers? Do we need to hire a DJ for our event? All of these—and many more questions—need to be addressed as you work toward developing and expanding your organization.

What Will Your Tactics Be?

The final question involves your actual actions and tactics. What are the actions you want to take to get your message across and solve the problem you have identified? Your tactics will depend on the issue and what is the end result you will be working toward. You need to think about who are the people you need to reach and what are the best ways to reach them.

Heather Booth shares the following:

> You take the answers to all those questions and you put them into a timeline, taking into account how much time you will need to accomplish each

The Midwest Academy Strategy Chart

Goals	Organizational Considerations	Constituents, Allies and Opponents	Decision Maker (Target)	Tactics
Long-Term Goals Your overall goal to solve the problem, reflecting your values and worldview. Example: All workers receive livable wages!	**What resources can you put in now?** • Number of people, paid and unpaid? • % available time? • Social media lists? • Mtg space, copiers, etc. • Money? *Be Specific! Use numbers!*	**Constituents/Base** • Who is most directly impacted? • What power do they have over the Target? **Allies** • Who else will be an ally on this issue?	Person with power to say yes to the intermediate goal! • Elected or appointed or corporate? • Do you have electoral or consumer power? • What will it cost them in money or political capital to say yes?	How you will show power to DM so they will say yes to the goals? **Tactics that exercise power over the Decision-Maker** • Letter writing • Petitions • Phone calling • Social Media Tactics • Group Visits to Target • Media Events
Intermediate Goals What you are trying to win in the current campaign. Example: $15 state minimum wage law. **Short-Term Goals** Partial victories toward the Intermediate Goal. Example: Get Rep. Smith to vote yes.	**How can the campaign strengthen the organization?** • Values-based unifying message • How many new members? Leaders? • Money to raise? • Public recognition *How much? How many? Be specific!*	• What power do they have over the Target? • Is that enough power or do you need to recruit more broadly, to find unexpected allies? *What messaging will help you recruit and motivate the people you need?* *How many? Be specific!*	• Analyze election outcomes / profits, etc. • Analyze your potential power over them very concretely so you can use it strategically! • What messaging will make target most nervous about the power you can build?	• Rallies, Actions • Public Forums • Strategic Civil Disobedience • Etc. – be creative! • Values-based message **Tactics that educate, recruit, build your organization** • Media events, etc.
Goals are always concrete improvements in people's lives!	**Internal challenges?** • How to solve/reduce.	**Opponents** • Who opposes this & why? • What do they lose? • What will they do/spend? • Can you neutralize or divide any opponents?	*Always a person with a name, not an institution!*	• Social Media • What's the message? • Teach-Ins • Rallies/Banners *Put tactics on a timeline!*

Check out this helpful chart from the Midwest Academy, which illustrates the steps one should consider when organizing for action. Try using this as a template to outline the steps you need to take when organizing your own strategy for action. © *Midwest Academy* one of these things and when each thing must be done, and that gives you a strategic plan.

You also need to know what you want to say about what you are working for. That is what many people call your message. Much research has been done—especially by the advertising industry—to try and determine how a message is best communicated and retained. And one thing seems to be clear, and that is that repetition works. So a favorite phrase of mine is, "Repetition is our friend. Repetition is our friend. Repetition is our friend."

Once you have a strategic plan, you can begin to implement it. You will almost certainly find that the path is not smooth, but that's when you begin to learn and to adapt. You may plan to hold a meeting for twenty people, but only five show up. That's when you need to ask yourself: Where did we go wrong? What can we learn from that? That is how you grow and how you develop a more successful strategy. You must be willing to learn from others, people who have experience to share. That's where I believe an alliance between younger people and older people can be a particularly strong partnership: when they work together and learn from each other—as long as there is mutual respect, genuine caring, and common values and interests.

To make change happen on a large scale, it is essential to organize—to organize people, to organize resources, and to organize a plan to put it all together. There are reasons to do it to make change happen, and there are reasons to do it for humanity. Organizing for positive change doesn't just achieve good; it helps people band together for a common cause. And that is good for everyone. As world-renowned chef, activist, and humanitarian José Andrés, who founded World Central Kitchen, a nonprofit that has provided millions of meals to people in the aftermath of natural disasters, eloquently said, "It's very therapeutic for people to activate, but they need structure. They need somebody to say, 'Hey, we could use some help.'"[13]

Chapter Five

Tools for Activism and Social Impact

There are certain skills, knowledge, and abilities which you can develop to help you become a successful activist or advocate; these become tools in your toolbox, ready to be used throughout your journey. Some can be learned from published or online materials; some can be learned by participating in workshops or conferences; and some can be learned on the job from watching, doing, and learning from others. There are, among other things, tools that can help you find people who can offer you guidance, support, and information—tools to help you communicate effectively, tools to find funding for your work, tools for research, and tools for making connections.

In this section, we will take a look at some particularly valuable tools and how you might acquire or develop them. Some of these may be tools with which you are already familiar and comfortable using, but there are others about which you will want to learn more, explore further, and learn how to put into practice. At the end of this book is a list of selected resources that can lead you to more information, websites, or organizations that can further your knowledge and expand your toolbox. But knowing what you have in your toolbox and developing confidence in using these tools will be important as you pursue your journey as a changemaker.

CIVIC ENGAGEMENT AND POLITICAL PARTICIPATION

There are two important areas which you should understand as you engage in social action because they are essential environments for activism. These are civic engagement and political participation. Social and political scientists with whom I spoke all agreed on one point: while activism has far-reaching benefits in terms of raising awareness about critical issues and motivating people to work together to address those issues, to get lasting policy change, you must do the long-term work—the work of changing the system—that comes through civic engagement and political participation.

Civic engagement generally means citizens working to make a positive difference in the life of communities and developing the knowledge, skills, values, and commitment to make that difference. Civic engagement takes place in many different ways and at many different levels, and there are opportunities for everyone to participate, no matter how young or old. Civic engagement encompasses such activities as volunteering within your community, writing a letter to an elected official, donating money to a local organization, and even participating in discussions about issues which impact your neighborhood or your community. In other words, it means being an engaged citizen, someone who cares about and is active within their community in ways which help that community. Young people are important participants in civic engagement because they often experience a community's problems firsthand, and they are often the first ones to call out a problem and take action to address it.[1]

Political participation is a form of civic engagement; it means engaging within the democratic process in activities such as voting and in other forms of political activism, taking part in and shaping the decisions which affect our lives. It is important to understand how the political system works in order to make long-term change. As one political scientist with whom I spoke has pointed out, shifting public opinion is a long-term game. For example, following the horrific shooting at Marjory Stoneman Douglas High School in Parkland, Florida, there was an extraordinary and almost overnight surge of youth demonstrations against gun violence that rapidly spread from Parkland across the country and to many places across the globe. Photos and videos went viral and captured the public's attention, leading to a demand for stronger gun laws. But the gun lobby and the people elected to Congress who have strong ties to the Second Amendment proved a barrier to movement for stronger gun laws. The lesson to be learned from this is that in order to move political action in the direction you want, you must replace elected officials with those who hold your views. Changing the balance of power involves such things as redistricting, getting people to run for office who are determined to uphold the views you share, and recruiting people into the party system so that they will cast votes to elect those you support.

Within the framework of the political system, even if you are too young to vote, you can still participate in the process by lobbying legislators, helping with campaign work, and engaging in other activities within the electoral system that can shift public opinion. *New York Times* columnist Jamelle Bouie has recently recommended the first steps for people wanting to be more active in local government: "The best first step is just to show up. In most places, simply showing up (with a few friends) is enough to have a real voice at public meetings or other forums. And if you organize those friends, write letters, speak up during public comment sessions and circulate petitions, you can begin to compel the people with power to notice you and listen."[2] Getting your message to elected representatives—the people who will be making the decisions—and getting it heard takes skill. But getting your issues on their agenda is critical to engaging the political power that elected officials wield and being able to take your cause further.

Even as a young person, you can reach out to your elected officials. You can find out who they are by looking online for your community website, your city or state website, or the Senate or House of Representatives websites. When you do communicate with your political

The term *lobbying* refers to when an individual or group of people (known as lobbyists) tries to influence the decisions of government. The term originated when people approached legislators in the lobby outside the legislative chamber.[*]

---

[*] Editors of *Encyclopedia Britannica*, "Lobbying," *Britannica*, accessed June 23, 2022, https://www.britannica.com/topic/lobbying.

leaders, whether by email or phone, it is important prepare yourself: know their name and title, know what their position is on the issue that you would like to discuss, and know what it is you would like from them. Are you hoping to get their vote about something? Are you hoping to get your issue on their legislative agenda? Would you like their attendance or signature or other form of support? Think through and plan your approach and what you would like to achieve so that you can present your concern clearly and concisely. Learn more about how to communicate with political leaders or anyone else in the section below on communication.

Making lasting change is a process. Civic engagement and political participation are both essential to making long-term change happen, and young people can—and should—take an active role in both areas. While protests and demonstrations and other forms of activism may call immediate and far-reaching attention to a cause, it is through the political process—the work of elected officials, the people with power—that lasting change happens; short-term gains can build into longer-term gains. Being active in your community and participating in the political process in whatever way you can are crucial ways to be an engaged citizen, someone who takes their role in society seriously and conscientiously.

As Heather Booth has summed up, "As we organize to make positive change in our society, in our world, we need to work at every level. That means we have to work from within the system, by which I mean that there need to be some people who will serve in positions of influence, in an administration, in a nonprofit organization, or even by running for office. And we need people to work from outside the system, by which I mean people banding together within their communities to take action. I think the strongest way to effect lasting change is to work both from the outside and the inside."

FUNDRAISING

Okay, so you're getting deeply involved in your passion project. Sometimes it seems like all your time—at least any time you have left after schoolwork or home chores—is dedicated to focusing on your cause. You've gotten a few other people involved, and you're beginning to fine-tune your message, learn as much as you can about the issues, and think about your next moves.

But things begin to get more complicated when you become more directly involved in working on social impact projects because you will find that although you may have started doing it out of passion and a willingness to throw yourself wholeheartedly into doing good, at a certain point, the need for money to support your activities becomes a matter of necessity. Although you and others may be willing to give your time without payment as volunteers to the cause, suddenly someone has to shell out money to buy paper for the photocopier you will use to print flyers, pay to rent a loudspeaker for your first rally, or hire a bus to drive everyone to a demonstration. Will you have to rent a room to hold a meeting? Will you have to print a slogan on T-shirts to give away or sell? Do you need to buy pizza and soft drinks to feed your supporters at a sit-in? At that point finding the money to move your actions further becomes your most important focus.

There are simple means of raising funds that may be familiar to you, but you may not think of them as fundraising for a cause. Think of the collection plate in church, coins for UNICEF on Halloween, awareness wristbands for organizations like LiveStrong, or Boxtops for Education. Every grocery counter seems to host a container for cash to help people with AIDS, autism, cancer, or cerebral palsy. A bake sale with the proceeds going to a homeless shelter or another community organization or toys donated to hospitalized children—all of these familiar methods are examples of fundraising for a cause.

Not all cause-related giving is in the form of money; there are other ways of giving that intersect with activism. Think of Locks of Love, by which kids and adults donate ponytails to children suffering from hair loss; cutting off your ponytail to donate it to a child with hair loss is a form of activism. Buying and wearing a T-shirt emblazoned with a slogan for a cause you believe in is a form of fundraising, as the cost of the T-shirt is (hopefully!) going to the cause, and it is activism because you are proudly displaying your passion for all to see.

Many times, early fundraising for a cause can start with very local, hands-on fundraising efforts: a bake sale, a car wash, a "teen for hire" to raise money for a good cause. You can be creative in what kind of event or service you will plan, and with volunteers to help as well as enthusiasm and energy, you can create a lively community event that brings in some funding for your next steps. Just make sure that your message—why you are raising money—is clear and honest and well broadcast.

Before you ask anyone for money—family, friends, or organizations—you need to think clearly about your needs and be able to assign a figure to what those needs are. Try to anticipate not only your immediate needs—printer paper or refreshments—but what needs you will have as your project progresses in the next month, several months, or beyond. You don't want to return often to the same people to ask for money for immediate needs; having a plan, an estimated budget of what your costs will be, will help focus your "ask." That kind of forethought and planning will also project a financial maturity that donors will respect.

For many young activists, their initial source of funding is their family; if your family is happy to encourage you in pursuing your passion project, they may be willing to provide some early funding. As Zoya Haq told me, even though her family was hard-pressed for extra cash, her mother paid for supplies out of her own pocket when Zoya first started her tutoring project. But not everyone has family who can or will provide money to support their work. That is when you need to look further for funding.

Many people—young and old—find themselves hesitant to ask someone for money, even if it is for a good cause. One thing to keep in mind which will help you be more confident in soliciting funds is that you are not asking *for yourself.* You are asking someone to help support a worthwhile cause that you are passionate about. Being able to effectively communicate your seriousness and passion, as we discussed earlier in this book, will help you make the case for support.

And if asking for money feels like a hard thing to do, it may help to *reframe* how you think about what you are doing in asking for support: you are not asking for money to support your work, you are giving someone *the opportunity to do good* by supporting a worthy cause. Many people want to do good, to be generous, and to help others; what you are doing is offering people a chance to make a positive difference in an easy way.

Reaching out beyond your own family into the larger circle of people you know—whether relatives, family friends, or members of your community—will expand your fundraising potential. But you need to consider carefully how and when you will ask for money and for what purpose it will be used. Any funder—whether a parent, a family friend, or members of your community—will probably want and is entitled to know exactly where and how the money will be spent. This becomes even more important when your needs begin to grow beyond whatever your grassroots support can offer. That is the time when you may need to look into formalizing your growing project into a nonprofit entity.

While the kinds of hands-on fundraising events mentioned above can be a good way to raise a small amount of start-up funds, as your organization and activities grow, you will need to go beyond that for bigger sums of money to support your work. That will mean getting more formal about your needs and your methods. As your project grows and you look to expand it further, you will probably need to apply for official status as a nonprofit, or charitable, organization. Nonprofit status enables charitable organizations to avoid paying income tax on the money they raise and allows donors, in most cases, to take a deduction on their own income tax payments. There are many rules and regulations which apply to nonprofit organizations, both in the application process and the ongoing requirements, such as filing tax returns. Becoming a nonprofit organization takes time, and the legal process required to gain nonprofit status can be complicated; however, many of the young activists with whom I spoke were able to

"A foundation is usually a nonprofit corporation or a charitable trust that makes grants to organizations, institutions, or individuals for charitable purposes such as science, education, culture, and religion. There are two types of foundations: private foundations and grantmaking public charities. The money from a private foundation comes from a family, an individual, or a corporation. A public foundation gets its money from many difference sources, such as foundations, individuals, and government agencies."[*]

---

[*] "What Is a Foundation?" Candid, accessed June 23, 2022, https://learning.candid.org/resources/knowledge-base/what-is-a-foundation/.

complete the process successfully. Securing nonprofit status enables you to approach foundations and other organizations for funding in more significant amounts than you can raise through your immediate circle. It is a serious step to take and will almost certainly require adult assistance and input in the process, but it can take your project to the next level and beyond, and it is worth your while to learn about and consider. There is much information about the process to be found online, and I have listed some helpful websites in the resources section of this book.

Usually, you cannot begin to apply for grants until you have successfully registered your organization as a nonprofit entity. A grant is a financial donation given to an individual or an organization, generally by a foundation, a corporation, or a government agency and usually for a specified purpose. To receive a grant, you generally need to file a formal application that will be reviewed before a decision is made whether to fund that project. Grant proposals—the way in which you ask a grantor for funding—can sometimes be as simple as a letter outlining what your project is, how much money you are requesting, and exactly how it will be used. But, in many cases, they are much more complicated than that, requiring specific information, background materials, and supporting documentation. Begin by looking online for more information about grants, grant writing, and what organizations might be supplying funding for projects in your area of interest. An excellent place to start is with the Foundation Center Library website; I have included a link in the resources section of this book.

> "A nonprofit grant, sometimes referred to as a fundraising grant, is a financial donation given to an organization. Grant organizations, also known as grantmakers, are the foundations, corporations, or government agencies that provide the funding for grants."[*] The grantmaker "grants" the funding to the organization and is therefore the *grantor*; the organization receiving the grant is the *grantee*.
>
> ───────
>
> [*] "What Is a Nonprofit Grant?" Kindful, accessed June 23, 2022, https://kind ful.com/nonprofit-glossary/nonprofit-grant.

As many young activists discover, finding money to allow you to carry out your goals becomes a critical—and time-consuming—part of what you do. Finding your first funders, securing that first grant, can be an exhausting and disheartening effort. The upside, though, is that once you do, it becomes easier to approach other grantors—you now have some added credibility because others have begun to support your work. And as your network grows, as you become more tuned in to the world of activism, you will begin to have more contacts, more information, and more leads about where to go, how to apply, to whom to reach out, and how best to do it.

Learning how other young activists went about raising money for their work is a great way to get ideas and suggestions. One of the most successful with whom I have spoken is Jamie Sgarro, cofounder of AsylumConnect. Jamie has been able to offer excellent insight into how he found funding and organizational support during the process of growing as a young activist. As Jamie explains:

> When I think about doing an early stage nonprofit, especially as a young person, as I was back when I was in the early stages of developing AsylumConnect, my advice would be to target fellowships and accelerators for early funding and support. It does depend on what area you are working in; for instance, if you are in education, you will find that there are many education-technology opportunities that don't just offer funding, they are also accelerators, and they pair you with business executives, presentations, that sort of thing. For me, I was lucky enough to get a Roddenberry Fellowship in 2019, which offered not only a $50,000 grant but also one-year tailored support, which was very helpful; they paired me with other fellows, some of whom were farther along in their careers, and

What is an *accelerator*? "A business accelerator is a program that gives developing companies access to mentorships, investors and other support that help them become stable, self-sufficient businesses."[*]

---

[*] "Business Accelerator," Business Development Bank of Canada, accessed June 23, 2022, https://www.bdc.ca/en/articles-tools/entrepreneur-toolkit/templates-business-guides/glossary/business-accelerator.

The term "pro bono" comes from the Latin *pro bono publico,* which means "for the public good." The American Bar Association expects that lawyers will provide a certain number of hours of legal services at no cost to people of limited means or nonprofit organizations that service the poor.[*]

---

[*] American Bar Association Standing Committee on Pro Bono and Public Service, "Pro Bono," American Bar Association, published November 4, 2021, https://www.americanbar.org/groups/legal_education/resources/pro_bono/.

they were almost more like mentors to me than just people in my cohort. And the fellowship also paired me with pro bono experts in fundraising, marketing, and public relations, so to have that sort of support was really helpful.

I had heard about the fellowship through my network, but I'd also found it just looking at grant opportunities myself. I was googling social impact LGBTQ+ rights, and I stumbled on it because LGBTQ+ rights is one of their issue areas. And since people I knew in the field had told me about it, I figured it could be a good fit.

Getting the fellowship allowed me to hire myself—to pay myself for my work. Everything I had done till then to start AsylumConnect I had done as a volunteer, so in 2019, I was able to become a salaried employee.

I also connected with the Urban Justice Center, a social justice accelerator in New York City, which paired us with the executives at the Urban Justice Center, a legal nonprofit which has been around for a long time. To have that sort of expertise and mentorship early in your career, that was just invaluable because, as a young person, you're not going to know everything, so to have people you can ask questions of, I think that's really helpful.

In the early stages of organization building, before the funding starts coming in, you really have to rely on volunteers. You really need to be able to draw on volunteer sites to find people; there are a lot of free volunteer-posting sites like VolunteerMatch and Handshake. Those sites can really help you connect with people, potential volunteers.

When we were starting AsylumConnect, our first engineers were students, and one of them, who designed the first generation of our website app, did it as part of her honors thesis, so she had a real incentive to work hard on it even though we weren't paying her. We found other volunteers through student clubs. You have to find ways to entice people to your cause. For me, especially in the beginning, it was always about who is going to help with this. How do you get the word out in a sustainable, pro bono way?

I would suggest that young people look for grants through student-run conferences, fellowships—opportunities that are geared more toward early stage organizational development. For young people, especially if you don't have a wealthy network, you have to be crafty. Our first funding was from a student-run competition for which we got a $5,000 grant. Then we won a $15,000 grant through Princeton University's Business Today Impact Challenge, and suddenly, even though we were still run by volunteers, we had $20,000 to spend on the technology, and that really got us started.

We've worked with young interns, and their roles vary in the organization. We try to keep them engaged and motivated with virtual coffee chats, where I do a presentation and then answer their questions. It's really exciting to see the passion that they bring, and it's not all coming from one direction; sometimes they're really passionate about LGBTQ+ issues, sometimes they're passionate about refugee issues, sometimes they're passionate about both. Some people are just really passionate about using technology for social good. So whatever it is, I try to foster that. Some of them want to start a nonprofit and ask me what it would take to do it. I try to be as transparent as possible, but I think the issue area for whatever kind of nonprofit they are thinking of starting will affect the journey. My experience has been with LGBTQ+ rights and immigration, but even with other issues, I can tailor my advice in ways that are relevant.

With AsylumConnect we were lucky in that we started small. We were able to pilot our project in Seattle in 2016, just starting in one city at that time, and we took an entire year to launch the pilot and see what went well and what needed to improve. This was especially important because of how vulnerable our users are; we wanted to test carefully and make sure it worked. Then in 2017 we opened in a second area—Philadelphia—working that out, making sure that the growth was really just incremental before it went nationwide. I think it was really smart to move slowly because we were doing the world's first platform of its kind. It was not a simple decision because there were so many people in need of it immediately, and there was a lot of pressure to make the platform national right away. But in hindsight, I feel doing that would have been a mistake because the technology wasn't ready. Given our experience, I would tell young people to be patient and work out any issues before you scale up.

Jamie Sgarro has some other suggestions about finding funding opportunities. "As for logistics," Jamie points out, "there is grant software and things that you can use to source your first funding, like Instrumentl—although that might be too expensive for a young activist starting out. It's almost $1,000 per year, but that's not $10,000 per year. So something like that could help source grant opportunities, but of course, it matters what age a student is and how experienced they are in grant writing."

Kakooza Hakim's story is also illuminating because it demonstrates how making contacts and networking can be valuable in so many ways beyond raising funds: "We had applied for a competition in the US; it was called the Diamond Challenge," Kakooza relates.

> We didn't win the competition. But during the challenge, one of the staff from Peace First was an organizer of the event, and when they heard our presentation, they came to us and said, "We have a grant which we give to young people, you should check out our website and apply for it," and that's how I got connected to Peace First and applied for a grant. I was surprised when Peace First informed us that they were going to invest $250 in our project. And then, after the initial $250, they came back and told us, "We're going to give you $1,000 because we believe in your project." When I got back to Uganda after the competition, I made sure to share the Peace First website with my fellow changemakers. Last year, I was asked to be an ambassador for Peace First, where I helped them train other young people to become changemakers and mentored them through their projects. It was really gratifying to know that there are people out there who believe in young people and want to support their work.

Hayat Hassan told me about her experience getting Kow iyo Labo off the ground. "Going through the nonprofit process and registering as a nonprofit just shows how much of my work is supported by people who are not me, how much it's a community effort. It's definitely not something I could do on my own, because I would not know where to begin. Essentially, the organization I worked with on my youth empowerment lawsuit offered to step up and got us pro bono representation to file all the legal documents to get 501(c)(3) status."

Hayat continues:

> In that sense, I think we were a little unconventional as a nonprofit in that we did not have access to many big grants—or even any grants—and

"To be tax exempt under section 501(c)(3) of the Internal Revenue Code, an organization must be organized and operated exclusively for exempt purposes as set forth in section 501(c)(3), and none of its earnings may inure to any private shareholder or individual. In addition, it may not be an action organization, i.e., it may not attempt to influence legislation as a substantial part of its activities and it may not participate in any campaign activity for or against political candidates. Organizations described in section 501(c)(3) are commonly referred to as charitable organizations."*

* "Exemption Requirements—501(c)3 Organizations," IRS, accessed June 23, 2022, https://www.irs.gov/charities-nonprofits/charitable-organizations/exemption-requirements-501c3-organizations.

all our funding has come from personal donations. We had a GoFundMe campaign for awhile, and a bunch of people donated. A lot of those people were directed to the GoFundMe campaign because of news articles I was in, so that was a huge source of funding. There was also funding from my community, parents who were grateful that their children got access to tutoring and mentoring. So those kind of individual donations have been a big driver of everything that's been happening for Kow iyo Labo.

In recent times many individuals and organizations have turned to crowdfunding to raise money to support their efforts. Crowdfunding means raising money through donations from a large group of people, usually through online websites. You may already have connected with popular websites like Kickstarter or GoFundMe and maybe even have contributed yourself if a friend or classmate has participated in a 5K run or other fundraising challenge and asked you to support them or their team. These can be successful ways to get a project off the ground or to raise additional funds, but there are various fees and requirements involved, so you need to look carefully at what they entail, and decide what might be right for you.

There is no question that as your work in activism and changemaking grows, there is a strong possibility that you will have to raise money to continue and expand it. Learning how to do that and getting accustomed to doing it will be an important part of your journey. Learning from other young activists, finding out what you can on the internet or in other resources, and enrolling in any courses, conferences, or workshops on fundraising for nonprofits will certainly help give you the tools and the confidence to do that with success.

NETWORKING AND A SUPPORT SYSTEM

Networking is a term you often hear in many different settings. Basically, networking means connecting with other people who share a similar interest or goal. You can find a network which already exists and tap into it, or you can develop your own network of people with whom you can share ideas, work on projects, ask for advice, or otherwise connect with to advance your interests and goals. In that sense networking tends to focus on building business or professional relationships.

A support system is a type of network, but it is one which gives you emotional, psychological, or even practical support. It is generally a group of people—they can be family, friends, or even people you have never met personally but connect with in another way who understand your journey, can sympathize with your frustrations, or cheer your successes, as well as offer useful contacts and resources. There are various ways to network and expand your support system, and being able to widen your network can bring all sorts of benefits when you are engaged in social impact.

Some young people have a ready-made support system on which they can rely when they are becoming involved in social impact or developing a project. For many, having a parent or parents who have themselves been involved in activism offers a legacy of information and understanding. For those who don't have a family with that kind of history or even family members who understand—or even support—the impulse to work for change, finding a support network can take some effort, but there are certainly many ways to build a support system for yourself.

As Katie Eder explains,

> From my own experience, one thing that's so important is having a community of young people who are doing it—whatever your work is—with you and having a support system outside of yourself, even

if it's your own family or your school or a teacher or people online. Just having some sort of support system is huge so that you're not just trying to do something alone. You need to find people who will be your cheerleaders when things are hard and also will help lift you up further when things are good; it's absolutely critical to have that support system.

Following her success in establishing 50 Miles More, Katie Eder's vision has been to help enable every young person who has the passion, the feelings, and the desire to impact change to have the resources and the support they need; she is fulfilling that vision with Future Coalition. "The accessibility barrier to organizing is very high," Katie told me. "When we started, of course we cared, and we were dedicated, but it didn't mean that we had some special set of personal skills. We just had a greater amount of access and opportunity to be able to act on those skills and be supported in the changemaking we were doing. That's something we want to share with other young people through Future Coalition."

Jonah Docter-Loeb initially relied on family who were willing to offer expertise or support. But, he points out the following:

There are organizations like Peace First that provide funding and [are] where you can also find a useful network. And then there's a whole eco-system of people virtually or in person outside of your own network who might like to help you. I'd say start with your school, and try to find teachers or administrators who might be open to listening to your ideas. Reach out to those people, talk with them, and you may find that they are willing to help you and offer their expertise. I found that people—adults—love to talk about their experience and offer advice, and that can be very helpful, so don't undervalue it.

As so many people point out, relationship building is a key part of growing as an activist. Forging relationships with others who share your interests, who participate with you, work with you, and believe in you, is a tremendously powerful tool. Networking leads to relationship building: when you are actively networking, you meet other people, and they may introduce you to other people involved in the same issues and activities. You begin to become known, to be invited to join other activities, serve on committees, and attend meetings or conferences connected to your interest. This is how you grow your knowledge, your connections, your experience, and as MC Hanafee LaPlante points out, increase your level of credibility.

CONNECTIONS AND COMMUNITY

The ability to connect with people is critical to activism and change-making. Connecting with people, being able to listen to them, respond to them with sincerity, and include them in your passion, is intrinsic to leadership, to influence, and to being able to mobilize people effectively. Connecting with people means respecting their opinions, making them feel valued.

For Zoya Haq, connecting with people is the most important thing.

> The biggest lesson that I've taken out of everything I've done is that you don't always need to do everything on your own. I've always been someone who's really independent about what I'm doing, and I don't like sharing it with people. But taking advantage of the connections that you have with people, with friends, with people in your community, people in your school, spreading the information with peers, with people in your community, and really trying to connect on a personal level with those people you are working to help with the issues that you're working to transform or to change, it makes you more involved in the work that you're doing, makes it so that the people you are working with know who you are and can put a face to a name. Then they are more motivated to support you throughout the rest of your journey. So the biggest lesson that I've learned is that the best way to make a difference is to go out and meet the people who are going to help you do that.
>
> Community building is very energizing. And working with other young people brings out something in your work that nothing else can, because you're relating to people who have the same worldview that you have, who understand where you're coming from and are looking towards the future in the same way you are.

MENTORS

A mentor is someone, usually an older or more experienced person, whom you look to for advice and guidance over a period of time. Usually, a mentor has experience directly related to the field in which you are interested, but they can also have indirect or life experience which might be extremely useful to you on your path to activism. A teacher, a spiritual leader, an advisor, or an activist or advocate with expertise in successful action who is willing to talk with you about your interest and offer advice and guidance can be an invaluable mentor.

Sometimes a mentor relationship develops casually; you might ask a teacher if you can speak with them after class about your project, or a guidance counselor or school advisor might ask you about your project, and the conversation develops further, leading to more meetings and conversations. A good opening in developing a mentor/mentee relationship happens when the older, more experienced person suggests that they would be happy to talk with you again or invites you to come to them at any time with questions or to let them hear about what you are doing. In such situations, grab the opportunity—the potential for developing a meaningful, helpful, and possibly long-lasting relationship with someone who will listen to you and offer advice and guidance is priceless.

More formally, you can approach someone you think would be a good advisor, and ask them directly if they would be willing to mentor you through the process in which you are involved. If you do your research and identify people within your field of interest who might be suitable mentors, you can approach them with an "ask." As Jonah Docter-Loeb has found when he has looked for people with whom to talk about his project, developing a network of supporters or advisors can take work and persistence.

For Jonah, that has meant sending out over one hundred emails to graduates of his school to try and interest people in supporting his project. While most of his emails did not generate interest, he did receive some positive responses, and he was able to set up a series of thirty-five– to forty-minute phone calls with some alumni, who willingly shared their experience and helpful advice.

When you are reaching out to people to discuss your ideas, Jonah has some specific suggestions based on his own experience.

I found that people like to talk about themselves, so if you are interested in speaking with someone, get them to talk about themselves: ask them about their experience, prepare yourself with questions to ask them, or come up with a question on the spot, following up on something they said. Listen to them, and don't just try to interject your own story. Be deliberate in terms of what kind of information you would like to get from them. Remember that they are giving you their time, so be respectful and strategic in how you use it. Having the chance to talk with someone who is willing to take you seriously is tremendously valuable, and you don't want to flub the chance.

When you are meeting or talking with a mentor or arranging to speak with someone you hope might become a mentor, be considerate in your approach. Be specific: suggest a brief call or meeting, at least the first time that you speak. For instance, ask if they might be available for a ten- to fifteen-minute phone call or a twenty- to thirty-minute meeting. Suggesting a specific length of time alerts them that you recognize the value of their time and that you appreciate their sharing it.

Prepare yourself for your call or meeting; know in advance what you hope to get from the meeting. Would you like them to share their story so that you can learn from it? Would you like them to take a look at the project you are developing? Do you want their help in discussing a problem you are having? Plan for the meeting: make a list of what you want to talk about and the questions you would like to ask, be prepared to ask follow-up questions, and be prepared to take notes. All of these preparations demonstrate your seriousness and your appreciation of their time.

"My biggest advice," says Jamie Sgarro, "would be to source your mentors right away. I don't think there's one central place you can find a mentor, but whether you're going to google in your issue area or [use] LinkedIn Connect—that sort of thing—I would say that people are typically willing to talk to young people who are passionate. I know that I get contacted a lot about LGBTQ+ rights and trans rights, and I respond to those requests because I am passionate about those issues. So I tell young people not to be shy; they're not doing anything wrong by trying to contact possible mentors in the field they are passionate about."

For Jamie, having a mentor was critical to starting AsylumConnect. "Surround yourself with advisors, mentors," he urges. "One of our first advisors was a Penn law professor who taught refugee law, and we were really fortunate to be able to go to his office and talk things through with him. I think if it had just been me and my cofounder, Sy, in a room trying to do it by ourselves, it wouldn't have been good."

COMMUNICATION SKILLS

You've identified your issue. You've got ideas. You've got passion. You know what you want to do and how you want to do it. But how do you let people know? How do you get your message across? Figuring out how to communicate effectively so that you get your needs met can be transformative.

Being able to express yourself effectively—both verbally and in writing—is a critical tool not only in making your voice heard but in getting your message across. Being able to articulate your message clearly to your peers, to your community, to elected officials, and to the media can be your most powerful tool.

Speak with Maturity and Confidence

One of the biggest challenges for young people who want to make their voices heard is making sure they get taken seriously. Much of what you will need to do to accomplish your goals will mean talking with adults and working to engage their interest and support for your project. And while many adults may be willing to listen to your pitch, you need to know how to communicate your ideas effectively so that they see beyond your age and recognize your capability *despite* your youth.

Being young is not necessarily a handicap; how a young person speaks and presents themselves, though, may be. There are speech habits and language styles particularly common to young people that may hamper their communication with adults, but you can learn to avoid them—to speak with more authority and clarity—and that will be a big step on the road to being taken seriously. It's important to know your audience and be adaptable enough to tailor your speech so that your presentation is appropriate to your listeners.

There are—or should be—differences in how you speak with peers and how you speak with adults, and knowing how to adjust your speech depending on whom you are speaking with is a useful skill to acquire. When talking with peers, for example, teens tend to talk fast—to use slang, to mumble or swallow their words, or to use verbal shorthand that they expect others to grasp. It's fine to talk fast and use informal language with your friends, but when you are trying to present as a mature, knowledgeable, and capable person to an adult listener, you should avoid the casual, slangy cadence you probably use with your peers.

One trick to sounding older and more serious is to lower the pitch of your voice. Younger voices tend to be higher—no matter the gender—and therefore sound more childish. Practice lowering the pitch of your voice; it helps to try that aloud, especially in front of a mirror. Try saying a simple phrase or even reading a paragraph, first in your normal pitch, or voice, and then try it again with pitching your voice a little lower. You don't want to make your voice sound artificial or theatrical; you just want to make it sound a little more mature. Practice doing that until you begin to feel comfortable using that lower pitch.

Another giveaway to learn to avoid is what is known as "Valley Girl speak,"[3] a style of speech satirized in 1980s and 1990s pop culture, including by Frank Zappa's hit song "Valley Girl" and movies such as *Clueless* and *Heathers*. It is a speech pattern characterized by "uptalk," a rising, questioning pitch at the end of sentences, as well as the frequent use of emphasized filler words such as "like," "totally," and "whatever." It has become a widespread style of speech even among adults, but to many people, it indicates superficiality. It can be hard to break speech habits, but with practice and an awareness of what you want to avoid, you can learn to adapt your manner of speaking to sound more thoughtful and serious.

Try to listen to yourself speak, and be conscious of the times you use those habits—and then practice trying to avoid them, or even learn to drop them from your speech altogether. Although this habit is not limited to teens, whether you are a teen or adult making a presentation or speaking seriously about a subject, it can be an annoying and disconcerting verbal tic, which takes away from the message you are trying to convey.

Use Thoughtful and Appropriate Vocabulary

Another aspect of communicating effectively is using vocabulary thoughtfully. Learn to expand your vocabulary anyway you can; reading is often the easiest way to do that, but games like crossword puzzles, Scrabble, Wordle, and Boggle are also simple, entertaining ways to learn new words and use them appropriately. But always aim for clarity and brevity, and beware of using overly florid or complicated speech or interjecting multisyllabic words when shorter ones will do. It is not uncommon for a teen to use an elaborate word in an attempt to sound knowledgeable or sophisticated and stumble unknowingly into using an awkward malapropism.

Activities That Enhance Communication Skills

There are various ways to enhance your communication skills; for many young people, participating in organized activities such as debate team, speech club, Model UN, or YMCA's Youth & Government programs offer many skill-building opportunities, including how to communicate effectively. Such experience proved a training ground for many politicians and other influential people: President George W. Bush, Congressmen Edmund Muskie and George McGovern, Congresswoman Barbara Jordan, Supreme Court Justice Antonin Scalia, and television producer and philanthropist Oprah Winfrey, among many others, all participated in high school or college debate.[4]

Participating in such activities teaches more than just speaking skills; as a recent article in the *New York Times* points out, "What do conservative political figures like Ted Cruz, Steve Bannon, Karl Rove and Richard Nixon have in common with liberal politicians like Elizabeth Warren, Andrew Yang, Kamala Harris and Bill Clinton? They all honed their skills of rhetoric, reasoning and persuasion on school debate teams."[5] Young people who participate in debate and speech club learn to use their powers of persuasion—to present arguments that are clear, concise, and understandable, even when they are complex. They learn to carry out rapid research, to cooperate with team members, and to be collegially supportive of others. And they learn to speak quickly, making points rapidly but effectively, something that can be very helpful when trying to pitch an idea in a limited amount of time. The ability to craft and present an argument concisely and effectively will boost your chance of being listened to, of being taken seriously. No one wants to listen to someone ramble or wander off point; being able to organize your message and articulate it clearly and quickly is paramount to being an effective advocate or activist.

There are numerous benefits to participating in such formal activities. As Jonah Docter-Loeb explained,

I started out in debate and transitioned to speech. I think if you have a club available at school, join it if you can. If your school doesn't have one but has the bandwidth to do it, start one. I'm able to articulate what's on my mind because of speech and debate. Speech and debate taught me the really important components of rapid research, of being able to find sources that confirm your thinking, or to find other people who are doing something similar within five minutes, just by doing a Google search. And speech and debate helped give me the confidence to reach out and go out on a limb.

MC Hanafee LaPlante also found that to be true. "I didn't actually do speech in high school, but for a lot of my friends who did do it, their public speaking skills were completely transformed. I think just learning how to talk to people and how to express yourself in a way that will make people want to listen to you is so important."

Listen

One often overlooked component of successful verbal communication is the art of listening. Listening is as important in a conversation as speaking. Whether you are in a discussion or answering questions following a presentation, make sure to listen to whatever the other person is saying, and allow them to complete their thoughts without interruption or anticipating what you will reply. This is not just a function of common courtesy; it allows you to hear and learn what someone else thinks, deepening your understanding of whatever you are discussing and broadening your own thinking.

Write Effectively

Learning to express yourself well in writing is also a skill; chances are your teachers have been helping you hone your skills throughout your school career. Take those skills outside the classroom into your life beyond. When you are preparing written materials—letters, flyers, informational materials—or writing an online blog or webpage, it is essential to write concisely, to the point, with correct grammar, punctuation, and style. Sloppiness in written materials gets negative attention and makes your work look slapdash and unprofessional.

For Jonah Docter-Loeb, communicating effectively using email was something he had to learn.

As a young person, especially as someone who was still in high school, dealing with adults on email was something basically new to me. I had no idea about the norms of email communication, about the expectations of response times, about writing a succinct email that is spaced out and looks like it's less text than it is—those were all things I had no idea about. Luckily, I was able to learn from Kara Andrade, my mentor at Ashoka, partly just by seeing how she structured her emails but also by how she edited mine.

Another thing I've learned that has been useful is that when I've come across the name of someone who is doing something interesting or has written something interesting or runs an organization that interests me, I try to reach out via email and ask to talk. I now know how to keep my emails very concise, usually no more than a few sentences, and I try to reference the personal experience of the person I am writing to so that they know that I have been careful to do my research and preparation. You can usually find good information about them in their LinkedIn profile. I also read someplace that midday Tuesdays or Wednesdays is the best time to send emails. I try to ask them about something relevant and ask to talk to them about it or ask them for advice. Just keep in mind that if you do send out an inquiry, you follow up when you say you will.

Whether you are communicating verbally or in writing, in person or online, you are presenting yourself and your cause to people you hope to engage. It is worth every effort you make to communicate thoughtfully; if you are confident of your knowledge, have practiced what you intend to say and how you intend to say it, and have considered your appearance and customized your presentation to your audience, you are well prepared to make your case, be taken seriously, and advance your action in the best way possible.

SOCIAL MEDIA SAVVY

One skill which young people have in great supply these days is the ability to amplify a message on social media; young activists have become very creative at using their preferred modes of communication to spread their message. TikTok, Instagram, Twitter, and (though used less often by young people these days) Facebook, as well as newer, ever-evolving sites, are providing platforms for political education, influence, and social impact. By sharing stories, debating issues, conveying messages, and engaging in conversation, young people are making sure that their voices are heard and that people are being educated on issues that matter. It is easier than ever to open an app on your phone and find instant access to social activism. However, while the ease of using social media lends itself to impulsivity; be careful not to respond to or initiate a comment too hastily. Be thoughtful in comments and posting so that you don't send out a message that you might later regret.

Using social media effectively can be a galvanizing moment for a cause. Social media can amplify your message way beyond your immediate circle, but you have to be judicious and thoughtful in how you use it, or it can backfire and create embarrassment or disapproval just as easily as it can create positive buzz.

Online activism thrived during the 2020 presidential campaign, and teens along with seemingly everyone else were swept up in its use. Teen online activism was particularly notable when teens organized to use TikTok to skew the numbers in attendance at one of Donald Trump's campaign rallies in Tulsa, Oklahoma. In that action, fans of Korean K-pop music "joined forces with TikTok users to troll the president by reserving tickets to the rally with no intention of attending."[6] As a result, Trump's reelection team boasted that it would fill the arena but found that only a third of the number they projected actually attended.

Hashtags are another way to spread your message, but there is an art to their usage. A hashtag (or metadata tag) is a word prefaced by the pound sign (#), or hash symbol. It is a way of connecting online conversations or content to a particular topic, enabling people to easily find more information or connections related to that topic. Knowing how to use hashtags effectively can boost your message proliferation enormously.[7] You can review some basics of hashtag use in the cited blog.

THE ELEVATOR PITCH

The phrase *elevator pitch* sums up a good way to understand how concise and straightforward your message should be. Imagine that you have gotten on an elevator with someone you really want to engage in your cause. You're riding together up to the twentieth floor—and you'll only have a few minutes' time in which to engage their interest. What is the shortest, clearest way you can tell them what you want them to know? Hone your message down to that brief "pitch," and practice it until it becomes easy for you to present at a moment's notice. You never know when the perfect opportunity might arise—those few moments in which to really get your message across powerfully, clearly, and effectively.

CRITICAL THINKING

Critical thinking is the ability to understand the links between ideas and the importance and relevance of arguments and ideas; to be able to recognize, build, and appraise arguments; to identify inconsistencies and errors in reasoning; to approach problems in a consistent and systematic way; and to reflect on the basis of your own assumptions and beliefs. Critical thinkers identify, analyze, and solve problems systematically rather than by intuition or instinct. In other words, a critical thinker is an active learner, not just a passive recipient or transmitter of information.[8]

Developing critical thinking skills can be very valuable in being an effective activist. You need to be able to consider all the possible consequences of different actions before taking action. How do you develop critical thinking skills?

According to Helen Lee Bouygues in her writing for the *Harvard Business Review*, critical thinking is a learned skill.[9] She suggests three simple things that you can do to improve your critical thinking skills. First, question assumptions: ask basic questions about what you believe, and consider alternatives. Second, think through things logically—is an argument supported by evidence? Do all the pieces of evidence build on each other to reach a sound conclusion? And third, diversify thought. Find ways to take into consideration the views of different people; this will take you outside your personal bubble and open you up to diverse ways of thinking.

Learning how to think critically without just assuming something or accepting something you hear or read will enable you to think more clearly about your plans, your actions, and your beliefs. And the best tool to learn how to think critically is already in your hands: reading, and reading widely and deeply, is how you learn, and how you develop critical thinking.

SELF-EFFICACY AND SELF-CONFIDENCE

Self-efficacy refers to a person's belief in their own abilities to face challenges and to modify their behaviors and actions to succeed in reaching their goals. It is not quite the same thing as self-confidence, which relates more to knowing who you are and accepting and trusting yourself. Self-efficacy is more about *doing*—feeling that you are capable of being effective. Feeling confident and effective is not a natural state for teens. But being able to develop a sense of self-efficacy and self-confidence will be integral to your ability to speak up for what you believe in, confront others who may not agree with you, and be confident in your determination to achieve your goals.

Zoya Haq has explained the following:

The hardest part, I think, of being a young activist is that it's easy to feel a sense of imposter syndrome at any stage in the process. When I started doing this, and I started when I was thirteen, I remember thinking, "How can I do this? I'm not going to be able to make any kind of difference because I'm so young." And that kind of follows you throughout the journey because even as you get older, you'll be working with people who are older and older, and you always feel a little bit out of place, a little like an outsider. But then you realize that, no matter what, if you're making even a little bit of impact, you deserve to be wherever you are.

I've always been pretty shy, but I learned to break out of that a little bit, and I found that when I began to just come out and say whatever I was saying—whatever I was pitching—and say it with some level of confidence, then I began to command attention. When you are confident in what you are saying, or pitching, then people are more likely to pay attention to you. And learning that at a young age allowed me to realize that if I sound like I know what I'm doing and can show evidence that I know what I'm doing, if I have proof and I have all these people who know what I am doing, then why should I feel scared? Why should I feel that imposter syndrome? I know that saying you should be confident is easier said than done, and it's not the easiest thing in the world to speak confidently, especially when you are the youngest person in the room and you're speaking to adults, but if you start pretending that you're confident, it starts to imbue itself into every part of your life. So I started with my family first: I would put on a confident attitude when I talked about my projects. And then I would do it with family friends. When I was talking about what I was doing, I would try to present myself with decisiveness, with confidence. And as I started doing that, I realized that people were listening to me, people were nodding their heads, saying, "Wow, that's really cool," and they weren't treating me like I was inferior or younger. And that started to translate and trickle its way into the rest of the opportunities that I've had. Pretending to be confident can go a long way.

Even if you are just starting out, even if you feel you have no experience, it helps to take a hard look at what you have already accomplished and take ownership of it. You *do* have experience, you *do* have accomplishments—you just may not be thinking of them as accomplishments. Whether your experience has been successfully organizing a group project in school or working effectively at a part-time job, those activities should give you an idea of what you are capable of achieving. Jonah Docter-Loeb puts it plainly: "Get on LinkedIn. Don't sell yourself short. Even managing a club at school or doing a bake sale is an accomplishment."

For MC Hanafee LaPlante, being taken seriously was one of the hardest parts of pursuing her activism.

I've always been fairly self-confident, but I did struggle a lot with social anxiety when I was younger. I had this inner confidence, but I hadn't quite learned how to express myself, and so I think that—especially in middle school—I was not taken that seriously by teachers and peers, and so I was just very quiet. But in seventh grade, I started breaking out of my shell and was elected vice president of the student council, which was a big deal, at least for me. With that, I started to gain some confidence in public speaking, and from there, it kind of exploded. I was able to gain the skill of being able to speak in front of large crowds and being able to give passionate speeches—and that's something I derived a lot of confidence from and which helped me grow. As I was honing those skills, I started to feel that people were taking me more seriously.

MC also offered a different route to building confidence:

An activity that can really help build confidence in communicating is doing theater. I loved doing musical theater, and I did it from middle school through high school. I found that doing that kind of performing and honing those skills over a bunch of years is a really great way to build your confidence.

Another thing that really impacted how seriously I was taken in terms of my work in the environmental field was that I had credentials. I had

interned for the US Environmental Protection Agency after my sophomore year in high school, and I was able to work with a lot of the people
who were focused on the water crisis in Flint, Michigan. I gained a lot of
knowledge from that, in addition to the science and ecology knowledge I
already had, so I had a certain confidence in what I knew. And then when
I started talking to the people in my community about changing some
of the regulations and rules, of course they were thinking, "Oh, here's
this young girl who's going to come in and tell us what to do, she won't
understand the economics and the politics of it." But by being persistent,
almost forcing them to meet with me and have these conversations, it
became very clear to them that I was very knowledgeable about these
things and even knew things that they didn't know.

I think there's no easy trick to making adults believe you, but you do
have to act like an adult, you have to think like an adult, and you have to
be on adult level of knowledge and experience, and that's really difficult.
But I was fortunate in that my environmental experience and scientific
knowledge gave me a lot of credibility, and that credibility builds on
itself. So while I was often the youngest person in a meeting or on a
committee, I didn't feel intimidated at all, because I knew that I had been
invited for a reason and that the adults clearly thought of me as a peer
and someone who was as experienced and knowledgeable as they were.
It's kind of an exponential process: as you gain more credibility, you gain
more credibility.

Confidence for João Pedro came from preparation. "I've learned that
if you prepare," he said, "and you put in the work, you study what it
is you want to talk about, it may be hard to do at first, but if you do, it
helps you communicate your ideas and develop your communication
skills. People will listen to what you are talking about if it makes sense
and if there's truth to it. And if there's truth to it, it is possible to actually do the things you want to do and to make a difference, even if you
are only in high school."

Being at Tilt Camp was an important step in building both João
Pedro's communication skills and his confidence.

At Tilt Camp, although the judges were already willing to listen to young
people, you really had to study a lot, do a lot of preparation, and really
practice your pitch. You have to think about all the questions you might
be asked. You have to really know the things you're going to talk about—
truly know them and truly understand them. You have to believe in the
message that you are delivering; it has to be something that makes sense

to you, and it has to be something that people can relate to—even if it is a problem that they personally don't have, you have to make it relatable. You have to develop your speaking skills; try to speak clearly, speak without hesitation, and just be ready to deliver that message. When you are confident in your ability because you have really put in the work and studied the topic, then people can really see that, and they can see that you care about the message that you are delivering. Sure, some people might not listen because you are young. But some people *will* listen, especially if you are delivering the message with quality.

Building that sense of confidence is not easy, but it comes from understanding yourself and learning to take pride in your accomplishments and strength from your values. Don't be afraid to let people know what you are doing, what you are passionate about. Speak with family, friends, and whomever you can within your local community. Develop relationships and encourage interest in your cause.

Heather Booth offers these wise words about confidence to teens who want to be active in social justice and change movements: "Have confidence that you *can* do it. So much of society tells us, 'You're not smart enough, you're not good enough, you're not pretty enough, you're not handsome enough, you're not tall enough, you're not thin enough, you're not *enough.*' But, in fact, believe in yourself: you are *more* than enough."

IDEALISM

Idealism is what drives many changemakers, young and old. According to the *Cambridge Dictionary*, idealism is "the belief that your ideals can be achieved, often when this does not seem likely to others."[10] While idealism is good, being too idealistic can blind you to being able to achieve things in reality; idealism can lead to tunnel vision, in which you only see one way to achieve your goal. A successful changemaker must be able to encourage consensus, balance their own goals with those of others, and recognize when one has to make accommodations in order to achieve a greater good. But idealism can be the flame behind advocacy and activism, so keep it in your toolbox.

PREPARATION

Whatever you are planning to do, have a *plan.* If you are hoping to get people involved in your work, be organized in how you prepare your message. Prepare your arguments; try to think in advance of all the questions you might get, and prepare your answers. You won't be able to think of everything, but the more you prepare, the more you practice, and the more you try to anticipate what you will face, the more confident you will appear and the more confident you will be.

It is often hard to say what you want to say when you find yourself in an argument or when someone is trying to push back at what you are saying. It is always valuable to try and keep your cool; try to organize your thoughts before you blurt out your words. You want to choose your battles wisely—don't react without thinking, don't jump to respond to every argument. Let someone who gets argumentative or belligerent say whatever they want to get off their chest. Respond if you must with care, thought, and solid information. And back off respectfully if you aren't able to overcome a bully's rant.

If you are planning to make a presentation, whether to one individual or a group, try to first record a video of yourself speaking or reading your speech; watch and listen to how you sound, and critique yourself. Identify habits you want to break or mannerisms you don't like. It is a good idea to time your presentation and see if there is anything extraneous that can be cut. In general, a presentation should be concise but inclusive; make sure you include everything that is necessary to say and nothing that is unnecessary.

When I ask successful young activists how they approach the challenge of being taken seriously, the same answer has been echoed by many of them: do your homework, and be as well prepared as possible. As Russell puts it, "Do your research, and make sure you have all the cards on the table." Russell also offers a good piece of advice:

> Once you can really poke all the holes in your project and ask yourself all the questions that people may ask you, then you'll be ready for when they really do ask those questions. I believe in being your own biggest critic—question the feasibility of everything you propose to do. Once I can do that, I know that I've covered all the holes in all the places where I may come up short. So coming prepared, being really ready to talk about your plan—but also being ready to hear criticism—is, I think, one of the

first steps to gaining respect, not just from your peers but from individuals who may be much older than you are. At the end, you want adults to think, "Well, this young person has really thought about everything we're asking them."

EXPERIENCE

While many of these tools are skills which you can learn, experience is something you gain by doing. As a teen, you may not have had the opportunity yet to work in social justice, activism, or organizing, but you can begin to involve yourself in activities that will give you more understanding and experience of the work you want to do. Working as a volunteer for an organization or event can be a great way to gain such experience and can have long-term benefits.

As an example, Heather Booth points out the value of working in an election campaign. "It is helpful to work in elections," she points out, "Because elections matter. And the people who run for office and are elected to office need skillful people to work for them." She goes on to suggest that being able to work in a campaign office gives you the opportunity to see how things work, how people handle themselves, and what goes on in an election season. Furthermore, having that close contact may prompt you to become more involved in local politics and, perhaps, even to want to someday run for office yourself. Working within a campaign office can give you valuable exposure and experience, and it may be the first step in a long-term career. "Young people have the energy—and the courage—to run," says Heather Booth. "And it does take courage. But they have to know how to put strategic planning in place in order to run; they have to know how to set up a plan, raise the funds, organize a staff, contact the voters, and especially how they intend to make change happen." Working in a campaign office as a volunteer can give you the opportunity to watch and learn—and gain experience.

As you develop experience, you also develop credibility. As MC Hanafee LaPlante has found out, the more she participated in organized activism and the more she participated in and learned from meetings and conferences, the more credibility she had when she spoke. Adults listened to her because they recognized that she had experience to back up her ideas, along with solid scientific knowledge.

LOOK THE PART

Your physical presentation is a form of communication as much as what you say or write, and it can be as important as your words. The way you are groomed and dressed can communicate such things as respect for your audience and respect for yourself. It sends a message about how you feel about yourself and how you feel about the people to whom you are speaking. It can convey your seriousness and how much you understand about your audience, or the people to whom you are making a presentation, so it is important to take care with your appearance.

If you are presenting a pitch to a potential funder, for example, be thoughtful about how you want to appear. It may seem obvious, but it isn't something all teens think about. Make sure your physical hygiene is good—that you look clean and neat and that your clothes are appropriate to the setting. I have seen a teen come to a meeting where he was to talk to a panel of adults about his project, and the young man was dressed in a wrinkled T-shirt with a profane slogan on the front, torn jeans, scruffy sneakers, and unkempt hair. While the young man had some very articulate things to say about his project and goals, it was hard to concentrate on what he was saying when his appearance was so disheveled. If he had been attending a protest march, his look might have been perfectly appropriate, but if he wanted to be taken seriously by a group of adults, it was not.

SELF-CARE

One thing that was echoed by many of the young changemakers I spoke with is the necessity of finding balance in your life—making sure that not only can you handle your schoolwork, chores or job, and the pressures of the social impact activity you are working on, but also that you take care of yourself. For them, it meant making sure to find space every day to do something that helps give you some relief, whether it is taking a walk in nature, getting some sort of exercise, or listening to music.

Zoya Haq puts the need for self-care into perspective:

I think the first thing that's important to know about working in activism is that it is a marathon, not a sprint. So it's important to save your energy—don't get burned out, don't try to do a million things at once. For awhile I was in a position where I was doing so much, and I felt so burned out. We young people who are working on building these movements expect these movements are going to expand over the years, decades even. So we need to save our energy for that marathon, rather than getting burned out. Making sure we take care of ourselves first and foremost is, I believe, a form of activism. Having self-love, making sure that you're putting yourself first, is crucial because if you're no longer on this earth, if you're too burned out to do anything, then you won't be in a position to help others.

I know it's especially hard to do, and it's advice I need to take myself. I know that when I feel there are just so many problems, so much I have to tackle, I don't feel I have time to slow down. But you always have time to slow down, you have so many years ahead of you.

I learned all this from—I don't want to say failure—but from personal experience. I'm the kind of person who, once I am working on something (whatever that may be), I submerge myself fully into it. And that becomes my sole motivator, my sole drive. That happened when I was deeply involved in Kow iyo Labo—at the same time as doing all this press and being busy with the youth unemployment lawsuit and also going through the whole college application process. All at once I found myself so tired and so burned out that I didn't want to do anything, even the things that I was passionate about. I found myself losing my passion for activism, for my work, for school. So for me, that was a wake-up call and something I'd want to pass along to other young people in this kind of work: If you're losing your passion, then you won't be able to continue your work long term. You have to preserve your energy, your spirit, now to keep up the passion for your work.

WILLINGNESS TO LEARN AND GROW

One refrain I have heard from many of the young activists with whom I spoke is that it is essential to have the willingness to learn, to listen to others, and to continually educate yourself. One way to do that is to surround yourself with people who know more than you in different ways and to be open to learning from them. As Jonah Docter-Loeb puts it, "There's so much nuance in the world of changemaking, everything is more complex than it seems."

MC Hanafee LaPlante explains how she learned a lot through modeling behavior. She puts it in the following way:

If you're taking a math class, the teacher might show a problem on the board and explain how you do it. That teaches you something, and so you practice doing it yourself. You may not be good at it at first, but as you practice it and maybe ask for help, you eventually understand it. Changemaking is not taught in school. But if you think about it, if it were to be taught, it would probably be taught in a very similar way. So what I would like to tell a young changemaker is [to] try and replicate that learning style for yourself. Find a conference on changemaking and go to it. Or, for example, if you're interested in climate change and the environment, there is plenty of information in the library or online. You can find free Zoom conferences or webinars, you can listen to experts talk, and you can learn about how they are changing their communities. And listen—listen to what they're saying—and then try it on a small scale in your own community. You'll end up making mistakes, but as you do make mistakes, you'll end up meeting people along the way who will teach you, and you'll keep going to conferences and talking to people, you'll join the Q&A sessions afterward and ask questions, and you'll eventually get to the level where you'll understand what other people are doing to make change in their community, and you can model it yourself.

Really, the biggest hurdle is just starting. I had no clue what I was getting myself into when I first stepped a little bit into the world of activism. But as soon as one thing happened, another thing happened, and once you get the ball rolling, it keeps rolling. Just get started, even if it's not something your friends are doing. Join an interest club, join an event in your community—just start. Talk to people, get help, and you'll find you start getting invited to participate in other things and learning more, and then you're started on your journey.

Resources

Hopefully, this book has given you some guidance into the world of activism and social impact, and motivated you to become further involved. As you make progress on your journey into the world of activism, advocacy, and creating positive change, you will probably find that the road expands the farther along you travel. There are many routes to take, ideas to develop, and connections to be made—and sometimes, trying to make headway can be overwhelming.

Following is a selective list of resources which can help you further explore the world of activism and social impact. While some of these programs or organizations are open only to people of college age or older, there are still many things you can learn by exploring them; even though you may be too young to participate now, they may help you plan what you want to do in the future. They can offer you information as well as lead you to other avenues in your field of interest. Use these resources as a starting point or to deepen your knowledge and understanding. This is a journey you can be on for your whole life, and it can enrich your experience and keep you engaged and learning new things for as long as you keep going. Ultimately, wherever your journey takes you, do good things and be proud of what you accomplish.

ISSUES THAT MATTER

If you would like to learn more about pressing issues that face the world today and where activism and social impact initiatives are both thriving and desperately needed, an excellent place to turn to first is the United Nations Seventeen Sustainable Development Goals.

In 2015 all member states of the United Nations adopted a set of Seventeen Sustainable Development Goals (SDGs), a call for action by all countries to join in a global partnership to end poverty, improve health and education, reduce inequality, and spur economic growth, all while tackling climate change and working to preserve our oceans and forests. The goals are listed below, and you can find much more about them on the website.

United Nations Seventeen Sustainable Development Goals

https://sdgs.un.org/goals

Goal 1: No poverty
Goal 2: Zero hunger
Goal 3: Good health and well-being
Goal 4: Quality education
Goal 5: Gender equality
Goal 6: Clean water and sanitation
Goal 7: Affordable and clean energy
Goal 8: Decent work and economic growth
Goal 9: Industry, innovation, and infrastructure
Goal 10: Reduced inequalities
Goal 11: Sustainable cities and communities
Goal 12: Responsible consumption and production
Goal 13: Climate action
Goal 14: Life below water
Goal 15: Life on land
Goal 16: Peace, justice, and strong institutions
Goal 17: Partnerships for the goals

GOVERNMENT

Learning how our government works and learning how to connect with local and national policy makers is integral to successful activism and advocacy on any level. The sites below will give you links and information to learn more about government structure and activities.

United States House of Representatives and United States Senate

https://www.house.gov/
https://www.senate.gov/

Learn more about Congress and state officials, and find out how to reach them.

Youth.gov

https://youth.gov/
Youth.gov is the US government website that helps teens create, maintain, and strengthen youth programs, offering facts, resources, funding information, and other tools.

YMCA Youth & Government™

https://www.ymca.org/what-we-do/youth-development/education-leadership/government
Youth and Government™, a national YMCA program, empowers students from every corner of the US by giving them the opportunity to learn about—and experience—government policies and methodologies firsthand. Participants immerse themselves in experiential civic engagement, debate issues that affect citizens in their state, and even propose legislation. The program culminates with teens serving as delegates at their state conference, debating bills on the floor of the legislature.

BUSINESS AND SOCIAL ENTREPRENEURSHIP

Ashoka

https://www.ashoka.org/en-us/program/ashoka-young-changemakers

Ashoka Young Changemakers (AYC) is a global network of powerful young people who are creating an "everyone a changemaker" world. A carefully selected network, each young changemaker elected has launched social initiatives, formed peer-led teams, and created solutions for the good of all while activating others to join in.

Tilt and Tilt Camp

https://www.ashoka.org/en-us/tilt

Tilt uses a peer-to-peer-based approach to provide young changemakers an experiential opportunity to better define and move the needle on the 2030 Sustainable Development Goals (SDGs). Ashoka and its partners launched a pilot youth-led Tilt Camp for young changemakers to advance the SDGs by reimagining, requalifying, and recertifying the vision for progress. During the program, young changemakers develop plans for advancing the SDGs and work with diverse partners, including Ashoka fellows and private companies, to implement them.

Virtual Enterprises International

https://veinternational.org/

Virtual Enterprises International (VE) is an educational nonprofit transforming students through authentic business experiences that prepare them for fulfilling, financially secure futures. VE offers programs that provide all students with authentic, collaborative, immersive business and entrepreneurial experiences. VE partners with organizations across many industries who are committed to empowering youth to own their futures.

Youth Impact Hub Program

https://www.unitedrootsoakland.org/youth-impact-hub.html

Youth Impact Hub Program (YIH) is a five-month social entrepreneurship cohort fellowship program that serves transitional youth ages eighteen to twenty-four in the Oakland/Bay Area. YIH provides start-to-finish social entrepreneurship training, which includes developing a business model, business strategy, business implementation plan, and pitch presentation. Fellows get matched up with a professional adult mentor with experience in launching businesses as part of the program. The program's goal is for all the fellows to develop and present their social enterprise proposals to potential funders at a pitch event, and sell/display their product/service at an end-of-the-year marketplace event.

STARTING A NONPROFIT

These websites will help you learn more about what a nonprofit organization is, what starting a nonprofit organization entails, and how and when one must file for tax-exempt status.

IRS tax exemption workshop: https://www.stayexempt.irs.gov/home/resource-library/virtual-small-mid-size-tax-exempt-organization-workshop

Donorbox 501(c)(3): https://donorbox.org/nonprofit-blog/how-to-start-a-501c3

IRS exemption requirements: https://www.irs.gov/charities-non-profits/charitable-organizations/exemption-requirements-501c3-organizations

National Council of Nonprofits federal filing requirements: https://www.councilofnonprofits.org/running-nonprofit/administration-and-financial-management/federal-filing-requirements-nonprofits

FINANCE AND FUNDRAISING

Knowing about finances, budgeting, fundraising, and philanthropy is a basic skillset for someone who is serious about starting their own social impact project. But basic knowledge about budgeting and managing money is important for anyone, no matter what they hope to do. Check out these sites for more information to guide you toward financial understanding.

Budgeting for Teens: Fourteen Tips for Growing Your Money Young

https://mint.intuit.com/blog/budgeting/budgeting-for-teens/

This site offers some good basic money tips along with leads to other helpful information.

MoneySKILL

https://movingstudentsforward.org/moneyskills-free-online-curriculum/

MoneySKILL is a free, online, reality-based personal finance course for young adults developed by the AFSA (American Financial Services Association) Education Foundation in 2002 as one of the first personal finance courses available online. MoneySKILL provides educators of all kinds (including parents) with a resource to create high-quality, custom, web-based personal finance courses. The curriculum focuses on a broad range of money management fundamentals.

National Council of Nonprofits: Crowdfunding for Nonprofits

https://www.councilofnonprofits.org/tools-resources/crowdfunding-nonprofits

This excellent site explains crowdfunding and how it works and offers additional leads to other sites for more information.

National Center for Family Philanthropy

https://www.ncfp.org

National Center for Family Philanthropy (NCFP) offers a range of programs and services to foster learning for philanthropic families, including webinars, conferences, and networking.

Instrumentl: Grants for Nonprofits

https://www.instrumentl.com/

This software will help you stay on top of all grant deadlines and keep your funding history, future opportunities, and more in one place.

AWARD AND FUNDING OPPORTUNITIES

There are many opportunities to secure funding to support advocacy and social impact projects, but it can take research and perseverance to find and apply for them. Similarly, there are awards for innovative projects or programs, many of which offer monetary prizes that can make the difference in helping a project get off the ground. Below are just a few, but looking online or in the library can open a wealth of potential opportunities.

Candid

https://candid.org/

Candid, an organization formed by joining the Foundation Center and Guidestar, two venerable partners in the world of philanthropy, offers research, education, and training to help connect nonprofits, foundations, and individuals to the resources they need to do good.

Foundation Center Online Directory

https://fconline.foundationcenter.org/

Explore issues and find funding opportunities and training through the library or online. Although access requires a paid subscription, many local or academic libraries subscribe to the Foundation Center online directory and offer its services to their patrons.

Peace First

https://www.peacefirst.org/home

The Peace First Challenge helps young people (thirteen to twenty-five) create and lead projects that address injustice in their communities through compassion, courage, and collaborative leadership. They provide grants of up to $250, digital tools, mentorship, and access to a global community of changemakers.

The Diamond Challenge

https://diamondchallenge.org

A global high school entrepreneurship competition, the Diamond Challenge is a catalyst that propels high school entrepreneurs to the next level through meaningful connections, resources, and transformative feedback.

The Diana Award

https://diana-award.org.uk

The Diana Award is the only charity set up in memory of Diana, Princess of Wales, who believed that young people have the power to change the world. Its mission is to empower young people to lead that change through a range of initiatives which unlock their potential, inspire action, and create opportunities, ensuring that no young person is left out or left behind.

Adolescent Girls Fund of the Global Fund for Women

https://www.globalfundforwomen.org/initiatives/adolescent-girls-fund/

The Adolescent Girls Fund provides funding to girl-led movements in underserved areas, accompanied by resources and support for national, regional, and global learning, strategizing, and networking among grantee partners.

LEADERSHIP DEVELOPMENT

There are many programs nationwide that train young people in the concepts and skills needed to become leaders. While many are fee-based programs, there are often opportunities for scholarships or reduced fees available. Search these sites to learn more about what is available.

Hart Leadership Program (Sanford School of Public Policy at Duke University)

https://hart.sanford.duke.edu/

The Hart Leadership Program challenges students to practice the art of leadership in public life. It offers Service Opportunities in

Leadership (SOL), an intensive, twelve-month leadership program for Duke undergraduates that combines academic study, research-service learning, mentoring, and leadership training.

Girl Up (United Nations)

https://girlup.org/

Girl Up, established by the UN Foundation, is a movement to advance girls' skills, rights, and opportunities to be leaders, as well as a force for gender equality and social change. Girl Up guides and champions girls along their journey from leader to changemaker with specialized programming on global gender issues and in organizing, advocacy, fundraising, and communication. Girl Up's leadership development programs have impacted ninety-five thousand girls through five thousand clubs in nearly 130 countries and all fifty United States.

National Teen Leadership Program

https://ntlp.org/

National Teen Leadership Program (NTLP) offers leadership camps and one-day workshops to instill important leadership concepts in young adults. NTLP offers three-day, intensive leadership camps on college campuses and includes motivational speakers, leadership exercises, small-group sessions, interactive workshops, and interviews with business professionals.

The Youth Activism Project

https://youthactivismproject.org/

The Youth Activism Project helps teens learn to become activist leaders in their communities through online trainings, mentorship, and networking.

National Organization for Youth Activists

https://activismyouth.com/home

National Organization for Youth Activists (NOYA) is a nonpartisan, grassroots activism organization dedicated to inspiring and empowering civic engagement for young people.

ADVOCACY

ACLU National Advocacy Institute

https://www.aclu.org/issues/aclu-advocacy-institute

The ACLU National Advocacy Institute's High School Program is a gathering of high school students (ages fifteen to eighteen) from across the United States who participate in a week-long learning experience for the next generation of social justice advocates.

The ACLU National Advocacy Institute's College and Community Program will prepare college-age students (ages eighteen to twenty-four) for lifelong engagement in grassroots organizing, policy development, and legal advocacy.

The Foundation for Healthy Generations Youth Advocacy Training

https://healthygen.org/projects/online-youth-advocacy-training/

The Foundation for Healthy Generations offers online youth advocacy training focused on the actual process of civic advocacy, including practical skills and knowledge, and promoting active engagement in civic decision-making systems.

YA-YA Network (Youth Activists—Youth Allies)

https://www.yayanetwork.org/

The YA-YA Network prepares young people to take their place as leaders in the fight for social and economic justice through training and leadership experience. Founded in the belief that young people in their collective power will rise up and address issues impacting their community as activists and organizers, the YA-YA Network offers programs online and in person.

ONLINE MENTORING

WriteGirl

https://www.writegirl.org/about

WriteGirl is a Los Angeles–based creative writing and mentoring organization that spotlights the power of a girl and her pen. WriteGirl matches girls with women writers who mentor them in creative writing. WriteGirl is a thriving community with two hundred volunteer women writers serving more than five hundred girls annually. WriteGirl produces workshops, panel discussions, and special events to help girls get creative, get through high school, and get to college.

Girls Write Now

https://girlswritenow.org

Girls Write Now uses writing as a vehicle to build real relationships, and offers holistic services for teen girls and gender-expansive youth from systemically disadvantaged backgrounds, mentoring them throughout high school, college, career, and beyond.

ORGANIZATIONS WORKING FOR CHANGE

There are many, many organizations throughout the world that are devoted to improving a myriad of issues. If you do an even superficial search online for an issue in which you are interested, you will almost certainly find dozens of sites related to your interest. Below are just a few organizations empowering youth to engage in advancing social justice and taking action in making positive change; by checking these sites you can learn more about how these organizations are addressing the challenges we face.

Advocates for Youth

https://www.advocatesforyouth.org/

Advocates for Youth works with young people who are leading the movement toward just and safe communities for all. The Advocates for Youth Student Organizers Program works with young high school and college student leaders who serve as activists, advocates, and spokespeople at the local, state, and national levels.

Amnesty International

https://www.amnestyusa.org/youth/youth-and-students/
Amnesty International Youth and Student Program involves student activists in the frontlines of protecting and defending human rights.

Alliance for Youth Action

https://allianceforyouthaction.org/
The Alliance for Youth Action is a national network of local organizations which bring young people together to engage in democracy as voters, organizers, and leaders to make the world more just and sustainable.

The Climate Initiative

https://www.theclimateinitiative.org/
The Climate Initiative (TCI) is a nonpartisan, solutions-based organization pushing for local, tangible solutions to a global challenge. The goal of TCI is to develop a cohesive youth voice that influences decision makers to embrace climate solutions by educating, empowering, and activating youth.

UNICEF (United Nations Children's Fund)

https://www.unicef.org/
UNICEF works in over 190 countries and territories to save children's lives, to defend their rights, and to help them fulfill their potential from early childhood through adolescence. The UNICEF Youth Advocates Program is a global cohort of young thought leaders and young advocates with diverse goals who are speaking out and taking action for children and adolescent rights.

UNICEF Youth Advocacy Guide

https://gdc.unicef.org/resource/2022-unicef-youth-advocacy-guide
The UNICEF Youth Advocacy Guide is intended to help young people navigate the various processes to advocate for change.

DoSomething.org

https://www.dosomething.org/us/about
DoSomething.org is the largest not-for-profit website exclusively for young people and social change. Using a digital platform, DoSome thing.org connects volunteers, social change, and civic action to make real-world impact.

WE Charity

https://www.we.org/en-US/
WE (formerly Free the Children) is an international charity and educational partner with youth involved in education and development programs in forty-five countries.

Change.org

https://www.change.org
On Change.org, people connect across geographic and cultural borders to support causes they care about. Change.org empowers people to start campaigns, mobilize supporters, and work with decision makers to drive solutions.

Global Citizen

https://www.globalcitizen.org/en/
Global Citizen is a movement of engaged citizens who are using their collective voice to end extreme poverty by 2030. On the Global Citizen platform, global citizens learn about the systemic causes of extreme poverty, take action on those issues, and earn rewards for their actions as a part of a global community committed to lasting change.

Community Change

https://communitychange.org
Community Change is a national organization that builds the power of low-income people, especially people of color, to fight for a society where everyone can thrive.

JOBS, INTERNSHIPS, AND VOLUNTEER OPPORTUNITIES

Human Rights Careers

https://www.humanrightscareers.com/
Learn more about courses, workshops, internships, issues, and careers in human rights.

VolunteerMatch

https://www.volunteermatch.org
VolunteerMatch is a platform to connect volunteers with nonprofit organizations whose missions align with their interests.

Handshake

https://joinhandshake.com
Handshake is a website designed specifically to help college students find jobs and internships and connect with employers. Check out the website and blog to learn more about internships and volunteer opportunities, which can be an excellent way to become involved in your community and gain valuable experience.

PROGRAMS TO EMPOWER AND CONNECT YOUNG ACTIVISTS

Future Coalition

https://futurecoalition.org/
Future Coalition is a national network and community for youth-led organizations and youth leaders. With a focus on young BIPOC, queer young people, and young people on the frontlines, Future Coalition works collaboratively to provide youth-led groups with the resources, tools, and support they need to create transformative change in our communities and in this country.

Close Up

https://www.closeup.org

The mission of Close Up is to inform, inspire, and empower young people to exercise their rights and accept the responsibilities of citizens in a democracy. It offers a variety of in-person and virtual programs to connect students with their peers nationwide and help create lasting communities. Through the virtual programs, students gain the confidence to discuss and deliberate important issues, understand different perspectives, and work together to build consensus and connection to their communities and the world around them. With the guidance of Close Up's experienced facilitators, students will come away engaged, inspired, and motivated to continue the vital work of active citizenship in their communities.

NewHopeU

https://newhopeu.com/en/5c1d3-frontpage/

NewHopeU is an online platform that provides areas for designing projects, creating teams, accessing resources and opportunities, and connecting with other young global leaders.

Learning to Give

https://www.learningtogive.org

Learning to Give offers free resources to help youth learn about their communities and how they can help others with their time and talent.

TakingITGlobal

https://www.tigweb.org/about/

TakingITGlobal is one of the world's leading networks of young people learning about, engaging with, and working toward tackling global challenges. Their mission is to empower youth to understand and act on the world's greatest challenges using the power of online community to facilitate global education, social entrepreneurship, and civic engagement for youth worldwide. TakingITGlobal offers programs, resources, funding, and tools to get inspired, informed, and involved with local and global communities.

Urban Justice Center Social Justice Accelerator

https://www.urbanjustice.org/sja-in-action/
The Social Justice Accelerator empowers up-and-coming leaders by putting the resources of the Urban Justice Center at their disposal, enabling them to leap over the hurdles of being an early stage nonprofit and get directly to serving their constituencies.

The Conversationalist

https://www.theconversationalist.com/
The Conversationalist is a community and content platform empowering young people everywhere to have conversations that matter, with the mission of unifying the world, one conversation and one voice at a time.

RESEARCH

Learning how to do time-efficient, effective research can be an important step in building your program, reaching the right people, and learning what you need to be a successful advocate. These articles can give you some good tips on research techniques.

"5 Ways to Make Online Research Easier"

https://kidshealth.org/en/teens/online-research.html
This article offers some good, basic information on how to do online research.

"The Webwriter Spotlight's 8 Tips for Effective Internet Research" by George Mathews, May 24, 2022

https://webwriterspotlight.com/tips-to-nail-online-research
Check out this article for some excellent guidance on how to do quick, effective online research.

WEBSITE BUILDING

Giving your project or program an online platform can be valuable—or necessary—to your success. While website design, development, and maintenance can be a costly endeavor, with some knowledge and initiative, it is possible to find some cost-efficient or even no-cost ways to do it.

Wix

https://www.wix.com

Wix is a free, cloud-based website-building platform with millions of users worldwide. The platform gives you the freedom to create, design, manage, and develop your web presence exactly the way you want, and it makes it easy for anyone to create a beautiful, professional web presence.

"18 of the Best Free Website Builders to Check Out in 2022"

https://blog.hubspot.com/marketing/free-website-builders

In her blog post, Caroline Forsey lists and explains the merits and deficits of some free website development platforms.

Notes

INTRODUCTION

1. Robert F. Kennedy, "Day of Affirmation Address," June 6, 1966, University of Capetown, Capetown, South Africa, in John F. Kennedy Presidential Library and Museum, accessed June 19, 2022, https://www.jfklibrary .org/learn/about-jfk/the-kennedy-family/robert-f-kennedy/robert-f-kennedy -speeches/day-of-affirmation-address-university-of-capetown-capetown-south -africa-june-6-1966.

2. Mary Pipher, "How I Build a Good Day When I'm Full of Despair at the World," *New York Times*, June 28, 2022.

3. Emmaline Soken-Huberty, "Five Types of Activism," Human Rights Careers, accessed June 18, 2022, https://www.humanrightscareers.com/issues/ types-of-activism/.

4. Editors of *Encyclopedia Britannica*, "Civil Disobedience," in Encyclopedia Britannica, accessed June 25, 2022, https://www.britannica.com/topic/ civil-disobedience.

5. "10 Ways Youth Can Engage in Activism," Anti-Defamation League, published January 17, 2017, https://www.adl.org/education/resources/tools-and -strategies/10-ways-youth-can-engage-in-activism.

6. Rosa Li, "Extra! Extra! Read All About the Newsboys Strike of 1899," New York Public Library, published May 25, 2012, https://wayback.archive-it .org/18689/20220313122715.

7. "Youth in the Civil Rights Movement," Library of Congress, accessed June 18, 2022, https://loc.gov/collections/civil-rights-history-project/articles -and-essays/youth-in-the-civil-rights-movement.

8. Craig Kielburger, "7 Easy Ways for Teens to Give Back," Charity Navigator Blog, published March 11, 2019, https://blog.charitynavigator.org/2019/03/7-easy-ways-for-teens-to-give-back.html#more.

CHAPTER ONE

1. "Teen Brain: Behavior, Problem Solving, and Decision Making," American Academy of Child and Adolescent Psychiatry, Facts for Families, No. 95, published September 2017, https://www.aacap.org/AACAP/Families_and_Youth/Facts_for_Families/FFF-Guide/The-Teen-Brain-Behavior-Problem-Solving-and-Decision-Making-095.aspx.

2. "Why Is Youth Civic Engagement Important?" Tufts Center for Information and Research on Civic Learning and Engagement, published 2022, https://circle.tufts.edu/index.php/understanding-youth-civic-engagement/why-it-important.

3. Lisa Damour, "Why Demonstrating Is Good for Kids," *New York Times,* March 12, 2018, https://www.nytimes.com/2018/03/12/well/family/why-demonstrating-is-good-for-kids.html.

4. Teena Apeles, "Youth Activism in America: From Armbands and Walkouts to Bus Rides and Voter Drives That Would Shape Our Democracy," *KCET Newsletter,* November 4, 2020, https://www.kcet.org/shows/city-rising/youth-activism-in-america-from-armbands-and-walkouts-to-bus-rides-and-voter-drives-that-would-shape-our-democracy.

5. "Why Is Youth Civic Engagement Important?" Tufts Center for Information and Research on Civic Learning and Engagement, accessed June 19, 2022, https://circle.tufts.edu/index.php/understanding-youth-civic-engagement/why-it-important.

6. David Wood, "She's the Best Answer to Donald Trump You Never Heard Of," *Huffington Post.* published May 13, 2017, https://www.huffpost.com/entry/heather-booth-trump-protest_n_5914820ce4b00b643ebc1531.

7. Jan Eliasson, "Young People Must Be Recognized as Agents of Change with Much to Offer, Stresses Deputy Secretary-General at Economic and Social Youth Council Forum," United Nations Press Release, published February 1, 2016, https://www.un.org/press/en/2016/DSGSM933.doc.htm.

8. Ellen Daniels, "Activism in Youth: It's a Good Thing," *UVAToday*, published October 24, 2017, https://news.virginia.edu/content/activism-youth-its-good-thing.

CHAPTER TWO

1. Sole2Soul, https://sole2soul.xyz/.

2. NAACP Youth and College Division, https://naacp.org/our-work/youth-programs/youth-college.

3. Print to Protect, https://www.printtoprotect.org.

4. Future Coalition, https://futurecoalition.org/.

5. Speak Up Green Up, https://www.speakupgreenup.org.

6. The Tahira Project, https://www.thetahiraproject.org/.

7. HiStory Retold, https://www.historyretold.org/.

8. Kow iyo Lobo, https://www.kowiyolabo.org/.

9. AsylumConnect, https://asylumconnect.org/.

CHAPTER THREE

1. David Brooks, "Everyone a Changemaker," *New York Times*, February 8, 2018, https://www.nytimes.com/2018/02/08/opinion/changemaker-social-entrepreneur.html.

2. Jessica Grose, "What It Means to Raise an American Girl Now," *New York Times,* July 13, 2022, https://www.nytimes.com/2022/07/13/opinion/american-girl.html.

3. "Empathy," *Cambridge Dictionary*, accessed June 24, 2022, https://dictionary.cambridge.org/us/dictionary/english/empathy.

CHAPTER FOUR

1. "Inspiration," *Collins Dictionary*, https://www.collinsdictionary.com/us/dictionary/english/inspiration.

2. Marshall Ganz, "Why Stories Matter: The Art and Craft of Social Change," *Sojourners* (March 2009): 16–21.

3. Dana Da Silva, "Music Can Change the World," *Africa Renewal*, December 2013, https://www.un.org/africarenewal/magazine/december-2013/music-can-change-world.

4. Tracey Nicholls, "Music and Social Justice," *Internet Encyclopedia of Philosophy,* accessed June 24, 2022, https://iep.utm.edu/music-sj/.

5. Nadine Block, "100 Years Later: 5 Timeless Lessons from Joe Hill," Portside, November 25, 2015, accessed June 24, 2022, https://portside.org/2015-11-25/100-years-later-5-timeless-lessons-joe-hill.

6. Nandi Bushell and Roman Morello, "The Children Will Rise Up," https://www.youtube.com/watch?v=J-2V65bWqhA.

7. Philip Trapp, "Barack Obama Shares Nandi Bushell + Roman Morello's Recent Song," *Loudwire,* November 11, 2022, https://loudwire.com/barack -obama-nandi-bushell-roman-morello-climate-change-children-will-rise-up.

8. "How to Be a Relational Organizer," *The Crisis*, March 2, 2020, https:// naacp.org/articles/how-be-relational-organizer.

9. Daniel Craemer, "Greta Thunberg: Who Is the Climate Campaigner and What Are Her Aims?" BBC News, November 5, 2021, https://www.bbc.com/ news/world-europe-49918719.

10. Robin Marty, "Mad About Roe? Here's How to Help Women Now," *New York Times,* June 24, 2022.

11. "The History of Community Organizing," University of Washing-ton, http://depts.washington.edu/commorg/home/the-history-of-community -organizing/. For more information on the original source used on this site, see Morgan O. Reynolds, "A History of Labor Unions from Colonial Times to 2009," Mises Institute Daily Articles, July 17, 2009, https://mises.org/library/ history-labor-unions-colonial-times-2009.

12. Midwest Academy, http://www.midwestacademy.com/.

13. Patrick Radden Keefe, "Feed the World: Relief Army," *The New Yorker* XCVII, no. 13 (May 23, 2022): 12–13.

CHAPTER FIVE

1. "Understanding Youth Civic Engagement," Tufts Center for Information and Research on Civic Learning and Engagement, published 2022, https:// circle.tufts.edu/understanding-youth-civic-engagement.

2. Jamelle Bouie, "You Ask, I Answer," *New York Times*, July 16, 2022.

3. Kristina Seleshanko, "How to Talk Like a Valley Girl," *Our Pastimes*, September 15, 2017, https://ourpastimes.com/how-to-talk-like-a-valley-girl-12 112279.html.

4. Northwest University Eagle Debate Team, "Famous Former Debaters," World Wide Debate, accessed June 24, 2022, http://worldcollegiatefriends .blogspot.com/p/famous-former-debaters.html.

5. Jonathan Ellis and Francesca Hovagimian, "Are School Debate Competi-tions Bad for Our Political Discourse?" *New York Times*, October 12, 2019, https://www.nytimes.com/2019/10/12/opinion/sunday/school-debate-politics .html.

6. Kalhan Rosenblatt, "A Summer of Digital Protest: How 2020 Became the Summer of Activism Both Online and Offline," NBCNews.com, September 26,

2020, https://www.nbcnews.com/news/us-news/summer-digital-protest-how -2020-became-summer-activism-both-online-n1241001.

7. Hannah Macready, "How to Use Hashtags in 2022: A Guide for Every Network," *Hootsuite* (blog), May 2, 2022, https://blog.hootsuite.com/how-to -use-hashtags/.

8. "Critical Thinking Skills," Skills You Need, accessed June 24, 2022, https://www.skillsyouneed.com/learn/critical-thinking.html.

9. Helen Lee Bouygues, "3 Simple Habits to Improve Your Critical Thinking," *Harvard Business Review,* May 8, 2019, https://hbr.org/2019/05/3-simple -habits-to-improve-your-critical-thinking.

10. "Idealism," *Cambridge Dictionary,* accessed June 24, 2022, https:// dictionary.cambridge.org/us/dictionary/english/idealism.

Bibliography

Bartoletti, Susan Campbell. *Kids on Strike!* Boston, MA: Houghton Mifflin Company, 1999.

Cullen, Dave. *Parkland: Birth of a Movement.* New York: HarperCollins Publishers, 2020.

Hicks, Donna. *Dignity: Its Essential Role in Resolving Conflict.* New Haven, CT: Yale University Press, 2011.

Hoose, Phillip. *Claudette Colvin: Twice Towards Justice.* New York: Square Fish, 2009.

Hoose, Phillip. *We Were There, Too! Young People in US History.* New York: Farrar, Straus and Giroux, 2001.

Johnson, Maureen. *How I Resist: Activism and Hope for a New Generation.* New York: Macmillan Books, 2018.

Klobuchar, Amy. Foreword to *Nevertheless, We Persisted: 48 Voices of Defiance, Strength, and Courage.* Edited by This Together Media. New York: Alfred A. Knopf, 2018.

Lee, Chanice. *Young Revolutionary: A Teen's Guide to Activism.* Atlanta, GA: YBF Publishing, 2018.

Leu, Lucy. *Nonviolent Communication Companion Workbook.* Encinitas, CA: PuddleDancer Press, 2015.

Robinson, J. Dennis. *Striking Back: The Fight to End Child Labor Exploitation.* Minneapolis, MN: Compass Point Books, 2010.

Rosenberg, Marshall B. *Speak Peace in a World of Conflict: What You Say Next Will Change Your World.* Encinitas, CA: PuddleDancer Press, 2005.

Yousafzai, Malala, and Patricia McCormick. *I Am Malala: How One Girl Stood Up for Education and Changed the World.* New York: Little, Brown and Company, 2014.

Filmography

Below is a selective list of some documentary films about young activists whose stories may inform and inspire you on your journey to making positive social change. They may be available online, through your local library, or on streaming platforms.

CRIP CAMP: A DISABILITY REVOLUTION (2020)

This groundbreaking film traces the lives of kids from a 1960s New York summer camp for youth with disabilities to the streets of 1980s San Francisco, where the disability rights movement exploded. These determined activists earned national attention with their demonstrations, got sweeping reforms passed, and helped build a movement that changed the lives of Americans with disabilities.

FREEDOM SUMMER (2014)

This film documents how the Student Nonviolent Coordinating Committee (SNCC) organized the Freedom Summer Project of 1964, the student-led civil rights campaign in which more than seven hundred student volunteers traveled to some of the most violent, segregated states in the American South to help local Black communities register to vote.

GIRL RISING (2013)

Girl Rising follows nine girls from Haiti, Nepal, Ethiopia, India, Egypt, Peru, Cambodia, Sierra Leone, and Afghanistan who face almost insurmountable obstacles in their determined pursuit to become educated.

HEATHER BOOTH: CHANGING THE WORLD (2019) (HTTPS://HEATHERBOOTHTHEFILM.COM/)

Watch this documentary film as a tool for community organizing and as a guide to mobilizing activism and igniting change. Heather Booth, a politically conscious college student who began her career in 1964 registering voters in Michigan at the height of the civil rights movement, became the go-to strategist for causes for women's rights to immigration reform and an advisor to leaders including Julian Bond and Senator Elizabeth Warren.

HOMEROOM (2021)

Homeroom follows a group of BIPOC high school activists in Oakland, California, who led a successful movement to get police out of Oakland Public Schools, while juggling the realities of the pandemic.

I AM GRETA (2020)

This documentary film tells the compelling story of Greta Thunberg from her solo strike for climate action to her recent voyage across the Atlantic to speak at the United Nations Climate Action Summit.

JOSHUA: TEENAGER VS. SUPERPOWER (2017)

This film documents the story of Joshua Wong, a Hong Kong college student turned political activist who leads a seventy-nine-day campaign to shut down Hong Kong's financial district in defiance against the

Chinese regime. As the backlash comes and the crackdown intensifies, Joshua leans in even harder and becomes the face of a movement.

US KIDS (2020)

This film follows the student activists from Marjory Stoneman Douglas High School who ignited the March for Our Lives movement against gun violence.

Index

About the Author

A former executive in book publishing, marketing, public relations, and fundraising, **Jean Rawitt** trained in geriatric education at the Hunter/ Mount Sinai Geriatrics Education Center and went on to develop volunteer programs for Mount Sinai Hospital in New York City. She serves on the Board of Birch Family Services, a leading provider of early childhood and school-age education and residential and community services for people with autism and developmental disabilities. She is also the author of *Volunteering: Insights and Tips for Teenagers*, *A Loved One with Dementia: Insights and Tips for Teenagers*, and *Friendship: Insights and Tips for Teenagers*.

CPSIA information can be obtained
at www.ICGtesting.com
Printed in the USA
LVHW050320150623
749783LV00002B/5